Off Nevsky Prospekt

Russian Theatre Archive

A series of books edited by John Freedman (Moscow), Leon Gitelman (St Petersburg) and Anatoly Smeliansky (Moscow)

Please see the back of this book for other titles in the Russian Theatre Archive series

Off Nevsky Prospekt

St Petersburg's theatre studios in the 1980s and 1990s

by Elena Markova
St Petersburg State Theatre Institute, Russia

translated by Kate Cook

harwood academic publishers
Australia • Canada • China • France • Germany • India
Japan • Luxembourg • Malaysia • The Netherlands
Russia • Singapore • Switzerland

Amsteldijk 166
1st Floor
1079 LH Amsterdam
The Netherlands

British Library Cataloguing in Publication Data

Markova, Elena
    Off Nevsky Prospekt: St Petersburg's theatre studios in
    the 1980s and 1990s. – (Russian theatre archive; v. 16)
    1. Theater – Russia (Federation) – Saint Petersburg
    I. Title
    792'.094721'09048

    ISBN 90-5702-135-8

Cover illustration: Finale of *Private Life*. Photo: Vadim Mikheenko

Contents

Introduction to the Series

The Russian Theatre Archive makes available in English the best avant-garde plays from the pre-Revolutionary period to the present day. It features monographs on major playwrights and theatre directors, introductions to previously unknown works, and studies of the main artistic groups and periods.

Plays are presented in performing edition translations, including (where appropriate) musical scores, and instructions for music and dance. Whenever possible the translated texts will be accompanied by videotapes of performances of plays in the original language.

List of Plates

Before we turn off Nevsky Prospekt
(In lieu of an introduction)

The worldly-wise claim that you can only understand something by comparing it.

So let's do just that. And before we turn off Nevsky Prospekt, let's take a stroll along this main thoroughfare in St Petersburg, comparing briefly what it was like quite recently, in the last few decades, and much earlier, at the beginning of the century.

A few years ago Leningrad (now called St Petersburg again), a huge city with a population of over five million, possessed little more than ten drama, three musical and three puppet theatres.

Pre-revolutionary St Petersburg, which was much smaller than the present-day city in terms of the scale of its residential districts and particularly the size of its population, had more than two hundred.

Nor does a qualitative comparison favour the present day, if only because the earlier theatres were extremely varied, sometimes catering for widely disparate tastes.

One of the main features of the relatively few Leningrad theatres, however, was their thematic and aesthetic sameness. This feature, so fatal for creative organisms, was the result of their overall and practically total dependence on the state, which subsidised their activities on one unvarying condition – strict ideological censorship. Very few managed even occasionally to escape from its iron clutches and create a unique work of scenic art. In their attempts to circumvent the obstacles set up by the authorities, the creators of the Leningrad theatre of the sixties and seventies even invented a special "Aesopian" language, thanks to which their fellow citizens could guess at the meaning of what was being said on the stage. Yet even these mediated "heart-to-hearts" were not common. For the most part the theatre remained slavishly dependent on the state.

Many eventually got used to this state of affairs, however, and reconciled themselves to it, preferring long years of vegetation based on solid skills (for whatever they lacked it was certainly not professionalism or technical mastery) to creative quest. I say this not as an accusation, but rather the reverse, fully aware that they had no choice. For in those days it was practically impossible to open a new theatre and even more impossible to close one. All this quite irrespective of the relationship which a theatre developed with the public (which was sometimes a very dramatic one indeed).

For the sake of comparison, we should bear in mind that in pre-revolutionary St Petersburg all the theatres, both large and small, (except for the handful of Imperial theatres) were private concerns, dependent first and foremost on audience response. Which explains the flexibility shown in running them.

In Leningrad miracles of flexibility were performed by the above-mentioned authorities (and not entrepreneurs), particularly in the formation of theatre troupes. The personnel question was always the trickiest one. The biggest headache for party officials responsible for the arts were the talented young people as yet untamed by anything or anyone. Each year a whole bevy of them graduated from the Leningrad Theatre Institute (or the Leningrad State Institute of Theatre, Music and Cinematography, to give its full name). Only a few could be hastily dispatched to the provinces (as far away from the capital as possible); for the most part, however, these young people were simply denied the right to work, supposedly guaranteed by the Constitution, and ended up unemployed.

Once every few years one or other of them was graciously permitted to put on one of a theatre's planned productions, but always only with the rights of an ordinary director, i.e., hardly any rights at all.

These crumbs from the authorities served a dual purpose. On the one hand, they acted as a kind of personnel filter and, on the other, they made it relatively easy to kindle a brief surge of interest in this or that theatre with the help of a new name. Yet these one-off invitations never brought the young actors or directors concerned any real fame. More often quite the reverse. A promising debut could mean the end of a career, as in the case of E. Shiffers, who had the temerity to stage *Romeo and Juliet* as a play about modern youth.

Tired of the endless and futile hanging around, many young directors went to work in the amateur collectives which existed in each local house or palace of culture. This produced the famous "Blue Bridge" of Genrietta Yanovskaya and Kama Ginkas, the "Four Windows" of L. Shvarts and Tatiana Zhakovskaya, E. Goroshevsky's "Theatre of Real Art" (all graduates and pupils of our genius of a director, Georgy Tovstonogov) and many, many others.

It was a poor theatre, not in the terminology of Peter Brook or Jerzy Grotowski, but in the literal meaning of the word. Yet this "poor" theatre was far richer than the official "dead" one.

An intense search was going on in it. Unique "products" were being created there, if one can use this term about the theatre. And not only in the sphere of new issues (which could not be tackled by the state theatres), but also in the field of poetics. The poor theatre spoke to its audience directly, without hiding behind innuendo and allusion or having recourse to the intricacies of "Aesopian" language. These theatres were centres of social and artistic non-conformity, which undoubtedly upset the authorities, but not excessively. Firstly, the powers-that-be could always ban a production, even an amateur one. And, secondly, they assumed quite rightly that since these productions were put on in makeshift premises (often only an ordinary room) and when circumstances permitted (once a week at the most), these amateur creations would be limited to small numbers of performers and spectators and, consequently, would not present a threat from the artistic or the social point of view.

There was one important reservation in all this, however. The amateur actors were not sufficiently professional to retain for any length of time what they had absorbed at rehearsals, with the result that many amateur premieres which aroused considerable interest very soon gave up the ghost. In an effort to counteract this, many studio actors decided to apply for admission to the Theatre Institute.

It was an unwritten rule for theatre officials, however, that anyone who had worked in an amateur studio (and therefore been exposed to non-conformist ideas) should not be admitted to the Theatre Institute. After being turned down for some specious reason, they were usually told to apply for the theatre faculties of the N.K. Krupskaya Institute of Culture, whose diploma did not grant the right to work in state theatres, only on the amateur stage.

At that time the authorities still had no idea how soon and how radically views on the status of the theatre would change. Nor did they suspect that by "lumping together" the recalcitrant they were actually creating a latent core of opposition, which was shortly to play a decisive role in the theatre's regeneration.

Meanwhile actors and directors who had graduated from the Theatre Institute and not found full professional satisfaction in their work with amateurs invented a form of creativity which was unprecedented in the history of the theatre as a whole. It was jokingly called "art for art's sake", but the official term for it was "independent works" (as if anything creative could fail to be independent). A group of unemployed actors and producers would get together and start rehearsing something they found interesting in a manner that appealed to them. They did this without any financial backing, fully aware that the production would never reach a large audience. The only payment they received for it was the moral satisfaction of two or three performances to the theatre-going public.

This gave us L. Stukalov's unforgettable production based on Aristophanes' *The Frogs*, V. Zhuk's theatrical "kapustniks" (a type of satirical revue), K. Datishidze's first stagings of plays by Ludmilla Petrushevskaya, who was persona non grata in official circles at that time, the first appearance on the Soviet stage of plays by Slawomir Mrozek, a writer who was banned throughout the Soviet Union, and the realisation of many other creative projects.

Very soon these previews of independent productions turned into one of the most significant forms of the city's artistic and intellectual life. Moreover an environment was created which provided nourishment for those who opposed not only the authorities, but also the regime itself. And this opposition was all the stronger because it did not resort to open political actions, but expressed itself with the help of emotionally loaded artistic images.

An encounter with any of the "independent works" (even if some of them were not entirely perfect) made a much stronger and deeper impression than anything offered by the official stage, which was sinking deeper and deeper into routine and stereotypes.

However good such a production might be, it never managed to move to a permanent stage. At first many people dreamed of this, but as time passed it became clear that their dreams were in vain. These "independent works" with the right to be shown to a narrow circle had been deliberately instituted by the authorities: they had agreed to this relaxation so that people could "let off steam" from time to time, thereby calming down to some slight extent the explosive mood of the intelligentsia at that period.

By the end of the seventies it was obvious that prospects for the Leningrad theatre were very bleak indeed. People with talent were beginning to leave, some for the West, others for Moscow and other places.

At the beginning of the eighties the city's theatrical life seemed to be sunk in a deep torpor. In fact this was not the case. The unemployed drifted off home and continued to write plays, without the faintest hope that they would ever be produced, "kitchen plays" as they were called. The play *Natalie* put on by Kama Ginkas, acted by Gvozditsky and now one of the best known plays about Pushkin, was born in the kitchen.

Work also continued slowly but surely in the amateur collectives, where the graduates from the Institute of Culture returned in the early eighties, the ones who had been classified as belonging to the underground in some way or other when they tried to obtain a professional training, i.e., get into the Theatre Institute. So now this self-same underground got down to work, not so much by hastily putting on plays (this refusal to compete with the state theatres was a conscious one by now), as by searching for non-traditional methods of training actors and seeking to reinterpret the relationship between the theatre and the audience, the principles of ethics within the theatre itself and other important considerations of a theatre playing to a closed audience.

It is hard to say how all this would have ended, if the country had not suddenly been plunged into "perestroika".

From all the eloquent speeches which, incidentally, were not reinforced by the passing of new basic laws, theatre people grasped the fact, first and foremost, that it was now possible to open new theatres.

Moscow was the first to start this new process, of course, since the government was just on the doorstep.

Leningrad, soon to be renamed St Petersburg, was in the second echelon, because it still had the status of a "regional centre" and could not make its own decisions, being entirely dependent on the Centre, i.e., Moscow.

New theatre collectives, which all received the title of theatre studios, began to appear in the 1987/88 season, and by the end of the following year, 1988/89 there were about two hundred of them. Nobody could give the exact figure (a survey actually stated that "they are innumerable").

The only thing clear right from the start was that the reasons behind this upsurge were extremely varied indeed. The kaleidoscopic quality of the rapidly changing picture made your head go round: not only ordinary theatregoers, but even seasoned theatre critics could not keep up with all the first nights... to say nothing of trying to analyse this "artistic outburst".

An actor from the Tovstonogov Bolshoi Drama Theatre took over a cellar in a house in Hertsen Street (now Bolshaya Morskaya) and set up a Refuge for Actors there, in which he tried, together with his colleagues, to implement some of his creative ideas that had been unacceptable to official theatres for many years. The Tomashevsky Refuge soon began to attract other actors and directors, and the cellar became one of the most interesting rented stages. And in a former kindergarten in Moskovsky Prospekt the Sharmanka Theatre (Tatiana Zhakovskaya and Eduard Bersudsky) opened its doors, with huge wooden "kinemats" instead of people as actors. People's Artiste of the USSR L. Malevannaya together with a group of actors from the Theatre Institute put on perfectly traditional plays one after the other. While next door a group of very strange young people, who had never had anything to do with the theatre before and called themselves the "Theatre of Unsolved Problems", chose not to put on any plays at all, preferring to stage all sorts of (mostly dubious, it must be said) actions of a political kind. There also appeared a large number of nameless brigades, which in the space of a fortnight or so would "cook up" some children's play and perform it two or three times a day wherever they had the chance. For them the theatre became a means of making money. But money was also made in more refined ways: N. Belyak went all over the place announcing his project for an "Interior Theatre" (the city being rich in unique interiors) and got some pretty solid support from high-up sponsors, but, as it transpired later, never got around to producing anything on at all. While the productions of the extremely original Osobnyak Theatre (Igor Larin) were offered to the public free of charge in the interior of what had once been a Communist Party "red corner" in an accommodation office.

This period even saw the appearance of some new puppet collectives, including the Kukla Theatre (E. Ugryumov) whose productions were originally intended for adults and not children. Its repertoire contained plays by Fernando Arrabal, for example.

The Union of Theatre Workers set up some Creative Workshops, which ideally should have provided an interesting launching pad for anyone with talent. You could just submit a well-argued application to produce this or that play and if the All-Russian Association of Creative Workshops approved it, you got a subsidy. But alongside these long-term projects there appeared theatre studios associated with individual singers or playwrights, rock-theatres and so on. It's quite hard now to remember all the different prefixes to the word "theatre" (even fashion-theatre) that cropped up in those days. The important thing is, unfortunately, that many of these new establishments had little or nothing to do with the scenic arts.

The "theatre bacchanalia" lasted about two years. Its only positive result was perhaps the final destruction of the ideological and aesthetic stereotype which had had a stranglehold on the theatre for so many years.

The severe economic crisis which developed in the country helped to sort out "who was who" in the revival of the Russian theatre. By 1992 only about twenty of the two hundred theatre studios had survived. A few of these had even acquired the status of municipal ones. There were some sad and irreparable losses, of course, but the studios that remained were the ones that had found the strength to become part of the studio movement, which stood for more than just a collection of theatre-studios.

The studio movement is nothing new for Russia. As in other European countries, it first appeared here at the turn of the last century, and its birth is usually explained by the emergence of what was then a new theatrical profession, that of director. This explanation is undoubtedly true, but it is not the whole truth.

Later, throughout the twentieth century, the studio movement was to reappear several times. Its active periods always coincided with major (sometimes even radical) changes in the way of life, changes to which modern civilisation is particularly prone. For it is only natural that changes in "life-style" should invariably be accompanied by changes in people's "language of communication". (To quote two of the most obvious historical examples: Japan before and after the atomic bomb, and Russia before and after the revolution of 1917.)

The theatre depends very much both on changes in "life-style" and the concomitant changes in "language of communication", because of all the arts the theatre is the only one that addresses contemporary audiences alone and cannot exist without the direct participation and co-creativity of these audiences.

The theatre is a meeting, insists Jerzy Grotowski, one of the greatest directors of the twentieth century. But a meeting cannot take place without mutual understanding, without people communicating in the same language (this refers, of course, not only and not so much to verbal language, as to the more diverse and multi-level concept of a "language of communication").

Modern psychologists tell us that about 50% of communication takes place on the non-verbal level. The people who took part in the St Petersburg studio movement reached an understanding of this in the late 1980s and early 1990s intuitively rather than by studying works on social psychology. Life itself suggested this choice of path. The most important successes were achieved in creating plastic imagery (with or without the support of a literary text, it made no difference). This is why we shall be talking precisely about productions of this kind, although they arose in collectives with very different points of departure.

What is more, the studio movement of today is composed of small theatrical collectives with a precarious social status. Nevertheless they can without any exaggeration be called laboratories in which highly complex experiments are taking place: the people here are creating new forms of artistic language for the scenic arts based on the new, recently developed norms of the "language of communication".

The life of these studio collectives is a risky business. This is only to be expected, because as in any experiment it may work or it may not.

Studio collective life in St Petersburg today is actually twice as risky, because it is complicated by the general instability in the country as a whole, which causes all sorts of additional problems of a non-artistic nature.

Consequently it is impossible to discuss the results of the artistic activity of the theatre studios in St Petersburg today, without a word about the conditions in which they are creating their new theatre. This explains why, apart from traditional forms of theatre criticism, the author thought it permissible and indeed essential to make use of untraditional ones from time to time, primarily interviews and talks in which the interviewee's theatrical and personal experiences interact.

The first of these is about members of the generation now on its way out, which devoted all its energies (creative included) to preparing the way for today's experimenters.

Never lie to yourself

Admirers of the acting talent of Sergei Dreiden (and of the actor himself, of course) had to wait for more than a quarter of a century before the magazine *Theatre*[1] deigned to publish his "portrait". Dreiden made his debut on the professional stage in the early 1970s, yet the first detailed article on him appeared in the second issue of "Theatre" for 1990. Its author, Marina Dmitrevskaya, had a good word to say about almost all the actor's major roles, even remembering his brilliantly acted part of the piano (*Concerto for...* based on Mikhail Zhvanetsky, director M. Levitan), a production which was removed from the repertoire of the Comedy Theatre, banned by the authorities with a stroke of the pen, and only shown to the public once or twice.

In honour of this actor's brain-child that died such a premature death the critic called her article "The Piano Returns", but the real excuse for writing it was the premiere in the late 1980s of *Mimed Scene* (*Nemaya stsena*), which was quite unlike anything that had ever been shown on the Petersburg stage before. Sergei Dreiden acts it on his own, but he wrote it together with the director, Varvara Shabalina. They both belong to what is usually called the "superfluous" or "not in demand" ("nevostrebovannoye") generation. A very bad term, in my opinion, because it suggests that we should feel sorry for them.

But why feel sorry for them, when we should really be feeling very proud of them? I am quite sure that their successors will envy them:

YES! – None of them had a breathtakingly successful career or became a public idol.

YES! – They acted and put on less than they could have.

YES! – They were always short of money.

BUT! – It was precisely this generation, this "superfluous" society, that created the genotype of the independent actor and director; independent of everything (the vicissitudes of politics and economics, everything, except their own talent).

If it weren't for this generation, there would probably not have been a revival of the new studio movement in the late eighties. After all, it would be naive to suppose that these studios arose simply because Moscow gave the go-ahead. "Okay, you can open up now, the age of glasnost' is here!" Not a single one would have opened, obviously, if

---

[1] Founded in 1930 in Moscow and for several decades the only "thick magazine" publishing material about the art of the theatre. (Author's note)

they had not been inwardly prepared by then. And inner preparedness is not something you can produce overnight. It takes years to develop and must be nurtured by generations.

So it happened (not by chance, of course) that one of the finest productions by Dreiden and Shabalina came at the very moment when the bans were lifted and an attempt was made to introduce the rule of law in our land of Freedom (for all sorts of freedoms, creativity included). But even if *Mimed Scene* had not appeared, it would be worth getting to know about the fates of the "not in demand", because without this knowledge it is impossible to understand the present situation.

The best way of understanding these people is to let them talk about themselves, say what they like as they like.[2]

A stranger among my own people

Sergei Dreiden

"I graduated from the Leningrad Theatre Institute in 1962. After putting my diploma away in the special box for such documents at home, I began to wonder what on earth I had done at the Institute over the last four years. Most of all I remembered dark winter evenings, lecture hall number two and our teacher Tatiana Grigorievna Soinikova, talking on and on... While I (to my shame!) looked at her teeth and watched her chew. Tatiana Grigorievna had diabetes, so every hour or so she had to eat something. This intrigued me. I was stupid, simply because I was young. There was no concrete need for me to try and understand any-thing, to acquire any specific skills. But for some reason I always imag-ined the future as something endless and wonderful. Goodness only knows why.

Most people thought I had got into the Institute by pulling strings, because a lot of the teachers there knew my parents well. My mother was an actress (a reciter) and my father a theatre critic.

This gave me quite a hang-up. The only time I managed to achieve anything was during individual lessons, when I was on my own with the teacher, just the two of us. Usually I just showed off and fooled around all the while.

I think I'm probably a bit afraid of people. So instead of giving them time to upset (or, even worse, insult) me, I start trying to amuse them, literally overwhelming them with my clowning around. I was typecast right from the start in my year as court jester.

---

[2] I took the liberty of recording the monologues of Sergei Dreiden and Varvara Shabalina, editing them slightly and also giving them titles. (Author's note)

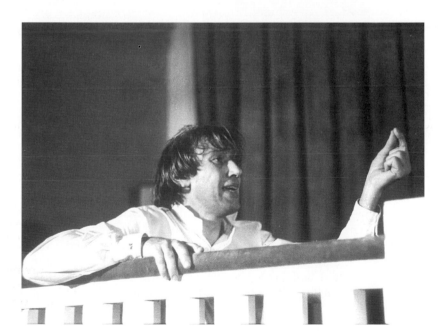

Sergei Dreiden acting Gogol's *Inspector General*. Photo courtesy of Sergei Dreiden.

Later, after the Institute, this mechanism went on working for a long time inside me. In the restaurant of the Palace of Arts, for example, where there were always lots of theatre people or people with some kind of theatre connection. I was never a heavy drinker. If I did get drunk, it was more from the crowd, and then I wanted to impress people round me by doing something crazy on the spot. I quite often did things that really affected my future just to show off. The decision to leave a theatre was sometimes taken like that.

The most productive periods in my life were the intervals between theatres. Left on my own, I would begin to educate myself like mad, reading, drawing and rehearsing for days on end some fantastic parts which were not (and could not be) in the plans of any theatre in those days. Only recently I realised that it was probably during these painful intervals that the main work went on inside me: the birth of my own theatre.

Actually I had known and enjoyed the atmosphere of being alone ever since childhood, because I was often left on my own at home when I was little.

Why have I always liked drawing, for example? Because you can draw when you like and as much as you like if you are on your own. All my drawings are done from memory. I can't imagine myself drawing something outside, where anyone could come up and watch you doing it.

I've told you a bit about how I fooled around as a student. But actually I always enjoyed studying a lot. When I decided to fill in the gaps left by my institute course, I went off to Arkady Isaakovich Raikin's theatre to "complete my education". And they took me – wasn't that wonderful? But four months later I ran away from there. I felt embarrassed about doing nothing (just walking on in crowd scenes) and being paid for it. Your financial worries disappear, but you seem to lose yourself too in the process.

Then I happened to meet Rosa Abramovna Sirota who was working at the Drama and Comedy in Liteiny. This was really good luck. Shortlived, it is true, because not long afterwards Rosa Abramovna moved to Moscow. At Sirota's rehearsals all the actors suddenly became themselves. There was no dividing line: now I'm an actor working, then my work is over and I turn back into being myself and go home. She was very aware of the human being inside the actor and able to help the two combine in a role. I had probably always dreamed of working like this with a director. After all, why did I keep leaving theatres, or the Theatre?[3]

---

[3] Dreiden also worked at the Leningrad Comedy Theatre with N. Akimov, V. Golikov and P. Fomenko and also, for a very short time, at the Sovremennik in Moscow.

The theatres where I worked were all run by different and, note, talented people, but the situation everywhere was the same: that of the average Soviet institution governed by its plan and its budget.

I could never understand why, if there was a bad premiere of a play at the end of the season, everybody still went on leave instead of staying to work on it. What's more, a month later, they would come back happily, sun-tanned and rested, and begin to perform this bad production just as before.

Who needs that sort of theatre. The actors? The audience? Why bother to put it on at all?

If you must work, it would be better to do so not in a theatre, but somewhere else, as a driver or something. Which I have done from time to time, when I went off "to the people", in an effort to stick to my principles by not taking part.

All that sounds very nice now, as I put it into words, but in fact it was not particularly nice at the time.

I don't know about other people, but I have wasted a lot of my life just waiting, particularly when I was young: in the hope that very soon (if not today, then certainly tomorrow) a director would be bound to notice me. And for a long time I couldn't understand why this didn't happen. Many of them came to see us at home (a propos of string-pulling) and had known me since I was in nappies. I had been skiing lots of times with Tovstonogov and spent hours sitting on Uncle Seryozha Obraztsov's knee!

When I got a job in a theatre I should have patiently and doggedly awaited my turn or chance, etc. No one was interested in me particularly. I should have reconciled myself. But that's precisely what I didn't want to do.

For a while I was saved by Leningrad television. They got together an interesting crowd in the drama department and the Horizon young people's department, and we took lots of liberties. When something worked, which it occasionally did, you felt dizzy with delight and thought that now everything would change, but nothing did.

I would probably have left the theatre for good if I hadn't wandered into the Palace of Arts in the late seventies and seen a poster saying: "The house is half mine". I was intrigued by the mysterious title. And seemed to detect in it a very familiar sensation of life.

So I went in!

It was based on a play by Alla Sokolova and produced by Ignaty Dvoretsky's drama workshop. I immediately came to life and felt that this was the place for me. Everything here was quite untypical. The theatre did not look like a big ship with lots of workshops and staff, which always put me off in ordinary theatres, where a vast amount of energy was spent on the entourage, but the main thing, the human touch, was missing. Whereas here not only the actor, but the spectator as well were regarded as real people. The actors acted very "lightly", in hints, as a result of which my imagination, as a member of the audience, filled in everything that was not on the stage.

In less than three years' time I was invited to take part in the same sort of production. It was there that I met Alla Sokolova, who was practically directing her own play called *Aplebuka, or Come in, Monsieur Chagall*. Her rehearsals reminded me of my meeting with Sirota. There was no dividing line between creativity and life.

We decided to follow this principle to its logical conclusion and got married shortly afterwards. Thus our family theatre was born, and then our son Kolya as well, who made his debut ten years later in the play *The Demon of Happiness* acting together with his parents. I experienced a whole period of quite inexpressible happiness when Alla and I were working together on the play *People, Beasts and Bananas* (*Lyudi, Zveri i Banany*). First we stayed at home (unemployed yet again) and simply wrote little plays. With time they developed into a long play like a mosaic. Each of the episodes had two characters which were acted by Alla and me, of course. The characters changed, but the actors did not. I think this gave the play the added meaning of how different human destinies can be.

We did not simply know the text by heart. It had been born from our contact with each other. We felt quite relaxed with it and acted it with great pleasure. Our performances were totally unrelated to so-called typecasting.

This "life in art" did not guarantee any social protection, but it was a real "high", as young people say these days.

I don't mean that, unlike many people, I think money doesn't matter. For example, I agreed to rehearse *Mimed Scene* expecting to be paid ten roubles for it. An actor was needed for one evening to act extracts from *The Inspector General* at an evening organised by the Theatre Museum. I was unemployed again at the time, so I agreed. At first there were a lot of us, then people gradually dropped out, probably thinking there must be easier ways of earning ten roubles. In the end there was only me, or rather, me and the director, Varvara Shabalina. This complicated things, particularly as there were only ten days to go before the great night. We couldn't expect any help. The museum could not provide us with a designer or composer, whose works so often accompany theatre productions. But the more complex the situation became, the more intensely our imaginations worked. I already knew that my fertile imagination could land me in all sorts of trouble. Then Alla saved the situation by suggesting that we should start and end the play with a mimed scene.

After that she did not take part any more in rehearsals, but her sugges-
tion decided our treatment of the play. So in the end we coped with the
assignment and, judging by everything, quite well. I played all the parts
in Gogol's *Inspector General* on my own. And we succeeded in creating
our own, unprecedented type of play: a rehearsal-play, where a great
deal depends on improvisation which, as we know, demands a great
mobilisation of forces from the actor.

Looking back I remember those ten days as a real gift of fate.
And remember Shabalina's direction with special gratitude, because she
didn't give me any instructions, but simply helped me work out how to
cope with this or that problem.

Since then I have acted *Mimed Scene* for many a season.

I don't want to upset anyone, but I cannot see any state theatre in
St Petersburg today for which I would like to act. True, Alla and I did
work for two years in the All-Russian Association of Creative Workshops
and it was there that the play *Demon of Happiness* was rehearsed. What is
more, I can say without any false modesty that we were on the verge of
opening our own workshop. But then the Association was suddenly
closed down. Why and by whom we were never told. There were
rumours that the premises had been leased to some foreigners to open
some fashionable baths there. It was a great pity. The All-Russian
Association of Creative Workshops was the only (legitimate) opportunity
there had been for many years in our city to search for something new, to
experiment, to take a risk. Then suddenly it disappeared for some
unknown reason and one imagined the following picture awaiting us
in the near future: foreigners arriving and going to the baths, while
Petersburg actors drift off home again to write their plays in the kitchen,
among friends, as before. So that's perestroika for you.

Whenever life gets difficult, I go back in my mind to one of
the strongest impressions which I had as a young man in the theatre.
These were the solo performances by the French mime Marcel Marceau,
whom I managed to watch twice by climbing through the window
in the gents. (It was quite impossible to get a ticket, even by pulling
strings).

There was this rather ordinary looking man and the auditorium
of the Lensoviet House of Culture packed with two or three thousand
people.

I shall always remember the total silence in the hall as the air
was filled with the most extraordinary radiant energy. Throughout the
whole two-hour solo-performance not a single person dropped the
inevitable cloakroom tag or coughed. So powerful was this performance
by the actor and the man.

Ever since then I have believed that the theatre is a place where miracles must happen, which only you can create, if you are capable of it, of course.

And that is probably all I can tell you about the ups and downs of my creative biography.

I don't believe in trying to predict the future. We shall see what we shall see. But to be honest I would like life to come up with more surprises."

Varvara Shabalina is the director of *Mimed Scene* which is acted by Sergei Dreiden.

Varvara Shabalina is more than just a name. It is a kind of password which can open up doors to any circle or group of theatre people. In the Petersburg theatre world practically everyone knows her. She is loved and hated, but people always go to her when things are hard, because they seem to know that she will always understand – whether its an unusual creative plan, or a difficult personal problem. Varvara herself, as director and actress, has had more than her fair share of trouble. She was always such a nuisance, you know, that Varvara!

Why is everything always so hard for us all?

Varvara Shabalina

"My problems began when my mother gave birth to me in November 1941. It was in Yaroslavl Region, where the teachers of the Herzen Institute had been evacuated with their small children. Apart from me my mother had three more mouths to feed. The first thing she did was to sell her beautiful braid of hair. Feeding a family was hard in those days, really hard. There just wasn't any food.

Then mother nearly lost me. There was an outbreak of measles in our house. The other children had had it, but I was only four months old. They wrapped me up in anything warm they could find, put me in a basket and left me outside in a temperature of forty-two degrees under, because this was the only sure way of preventing me from catching measles – by leaving me in the frost. She found me next to the stove of some men from the village (my face covered in cockroaches!). "Give me back my daughter!" she cried. And they answered back (tipsily): "Ee, you … Leningrad lass, what d'you mean by leavin' the kiddy out in the frost?"

What was the point of trying to explain to them?

At the same time my grandmother Varvara Stepanovna was organising a puppet theatre with the blockade children in St Petersburg.

As the daughter of Yevtikhy Pavolovich Karpov, who has been in charge of the Imperial theatre, she refused point – blank to leave her native city. She was actually the finest woman in our family.

She lived in Vtoraya Krasnoarmeiskaya (which used to be called Vtoraya rota) where she took in some children who were homeless and without parents. She got in touch with the authorities to help her feed her waifs and strays. There were eighteen of them altogether. Grandma had some big trunks of clothes. So they decided to start a puppet theatre. They spent days on end sawing and sewing, which made the bombing seem less frightening. My mother's still got one of the puppets they made, a little black boy.

Then one day a bomb fell on the house and set it on fire. And just imagine, the children carried all Grandma's mahogany furniture and lots of other things including the piano from the fourth floor down to the yard. And they spent the night in a corner on the ground floor. The next morning turned out to be even worse than the bombing – all the furniture had disappeared. Grandma died not long afterwards, from rage, I think. And the children drifted away…

After the war, when Father came back, wearing a captain's uniform with his pistol not handed in, we scoured all the flats in the district and found everything (tables, cupboards, etc.) except the one item we really wanted, the trunk containing Yevtikhy Karpov's correspondence with Vera Fydorovna Komissarzhevskaya. My parents are both historians and losing the trunk upset them most of all. But no one owned up. They probably burnt it during the blockade to keep warm. And who's to blame them.

My father had read those letters and told us a lot about them later. They sounded quite fantastic. The "Correspondence of Karpov with Komissarzhevskaya" that has just come out is only a fraction of what there was. So we lost something really valuable that could never be replaced and for no reason at all, that's the main thing.

When I was a bit older I went to study at the TYuT under Matvei Grigorievich Dubrovin. He was a really wonderful person. I was very fond of him because he noticed me straightaway and gave me a part. It was Dusya in Mikhail Svetlov's play *Twenty Years Later*. I had to sing "Transvaal, Transvaal, my country, you're burning in the flames!"

After my first taste of success in the theatre, I soon found out what hatred is like in the theatre.

TYuT had so-called self-management and a soviet (council) of some sort, like you had to have in our country in those days. There was also the principle that "labour education is the basis of talent", which meant that for the first few years you had to do menial jobs, like washing the floor, making tea, planing wood, etc., and only then you might be allowed to go onto the stage and act something. But Dubrovin gave me a part straightaway, and kept telling everyone what a wonderful actress I was!

And then of all things to happen Matvei Grigorievich went and died soon afterwards. And immediately, literally straightaway, the soviet which included V. Filshtinsky and Lev Dodin (our present bosses) threw me out of TYuT. And later tried to justify it by saying that I was anti-semitic. It all happened in the summer. TYuT had its own house in Skreblovo, near Luga. We were picking strawberries and spreading the newly mown grass. They made mincemeat of me, then gave me 5 copecks for my fare, so I packed my rucksack and went off to Petersburg. I was in my last year at school then, the tenth class.

Looking back on this later was a real joke, especially when I started getting summoned to "talks" by the "security organs" a few years later because of my husband, who happened to be a Jew and a dissident into the bargain. At these talks they tried to set me against "those bloody Jews", by which time I had a son, Danechka, a pretty little Jewish boy. Danechka's father later emigrated to America, but my son and I stayed here. It must have been Grandma's example.

My getting into the Theatre Institute and studying there were full of adventures.

After school I worked on props in the Komissarzhevskaya Theatre for a couple of years. Emma Popova and Alisa Freindlikh kept on at me to go to the institute. "You must," they said, "you're a born actress!" So I went along and in the office where they put your name down for an interview to get into the acting faculty they said to me: "Have you ever looked at yourself in the mirror?" I burst into tears and went out. The next day Emma Popova took me by the hand and put my name down herself. That year Boris Vulfovich Zon was interviewing. He was doing the work of three people, choosing students for his own course and also for Gorbachev and Time. He took Natasha Tenyakova and me for his course straightaway. But to my great misfortune in the third round, when we were acting short scenes, the elderly Time (God rest her soul) wandered in with Igor Olegovich.

My partner on that occasion was Ryndin, a shortish young man with an excellent bearing (he had just finished national service), and there was I, all ninety kilos of me, with my height. We were acting a scene from *The Wedding of Balzamin*. I bounced onto the stage, like the big round loaf in the Russian fairy tale to meet my young man with the stiff upper lip and said "Do you feel love?" – "Yes, ma'am", he replied.

And that was the end of it! Everyone was creased up with laughter, and we couldn't act anymore.

Igor Olegovich nicknamed me "Aunty Katya Korchagina-Alexandrovskaya" on the spot. I remember being offended by this in my ignorance and saying that my real name was Varvara. Elizaveta Ivanovna also made a speech, announcing to Zon: "You can take who you like, but give me Shabalina." (What she actually said was "this one"). So he did, because he had no choice. For one thing, no one could disagree with Time; and for another, he was a "cosmopolitan".

So that was the piece of bad luck that marked the beginning of my trials and tribulations at our Theatre Institute, where I actually studied three times, you could say.

At first everything was fine. By the third year I was already "classified" with the outstanding actresses, because I had acted in the theatre while I was still a student (the cleaning woman Dusya in Arbuzov's *Tanya* with Alisa Freindlikh in the main role in Vladimirov's production at the Lensoviet Theatre.)

Then suddenly the critic Khmelnitskaya published a review of this production (and not just any old where, but in Leningradskaya Pravda, i.e., the city's leading Party newspaper). The article was well-disposed on the whole, and the critic found something nice to say about everyone. About me it said that although Varvara Shabalina who played Dusya was still a student, her acting was as natural and the character she had created as authentic as in the case of the leading roles.

After this publication everyone started congratulating me and predicting that I would have a great future. But then the plot took a different turn. They took the part away from me, and threw me out of the theatre. Not at once, of course, but nice and quietly, when a good excuse turned up.

The excuse was not long in appearing. Before they threw me out of the theatre, I was also thrown out of the Institute, where a campaign against "cosmopolitanism" was getting under way at that particular moment.

Our syllabus included a subject called "individual lessons on stage speech". It was taught by a certain Zinaida Vasilievna Sovkova, who also happened to be the Party organiser at the institute.

When she and I met up one day for our "individual lesson" she began trying to enlist my support, as it was called, against the Jews! I was quite highly thought of at the Institute. *Leningrad Pravda* had written about me, but the main thing was that I had always been fat and red-cheeked, a typical Russian girl, in other words. Zinaida was extremely frank, particularly in trying to set me against Boris Zon. I pretended not to understand, so as to make her be even more explicit. When she asked me for a definite answer, I said: "What a pity we're alone and no one will see me slap your face". And I really did give her a slap in the face, and spat as well!

At that moment I was absolutely sure not only that I was right, but also that my (honest and noble) action would not only remain unpunished, but receive support in the eyes of others too. After all, I was one of the top students with a special grant, the head of my year, a wonderful actress who had already acted in the theatre. And, finally, I was very active in voluntary work as well, because I published a "cultural journal" in which Tanya Galushko (our poetess now deceased) wrote long screeds on Pushkin's unknown verse, for example.

But my head was soon to fall.

"They" organised a simple provocation. There was a girl called Lyalya in our year (she committed suicide shortly afterward by throwing herself down the stair-well from the fifth floor and getting smashed to pieces). Lyalya got up, poor thing, and said that an art book of hers (with reproductions of Rodin, which was unique at that time) had disappeared during the acting skills lesson. They started to search through our personal belongings, and the book was found in my bag, of course. This was all "they" actually needed to throw me out, but I helped "them" a lot too. My fury at this mean trick plus my artistic temperament made me scream out: "You dirty bastards! Mediocrities! I already work in the theatre, but you'll die in Flyshitville… F … the lot of you!"

And this was in the presence of that dear old lady Elizaveta Ivanovna Time, the noblest of souls. The only thing she begged me to do later was to apologise to the other students for using such language.

The rector's decision to expel me "for insulting her fellow-students" appeared on the notice board. The Lensoviet Theatre also dismissed me, announcing that there's no smoke without fire.

But when he heard about all this unpleasantness, "Uncle Zhenya" (Lebedev, People's Artiste of the USSR) announced quite simply and intelligently: "B … the lot of them", and took me onto his course. So I lost a year and began to study at our delightful institute for the second time. And finally got an acting diploma signed by Lebedev and Tovstonogov. And, like most of our graduates in those days, eventually ended up unemployed, although we acted a great deal. There was a rather funny form of activity in those days called "independent works". You rehearsed and rehearsed, then put on a couple of performances for theatre-lovers at the All-Union Theatre Society, and that was that! But some of the things that were put on would have made the state theatres' hair stand on end. I thought this was great: acting without being pushed around by anyone, even if it was unpaid. And it was convenient because I was living not far from the Palace of Arts in Rubinshtein Street. One day I was running along the Nevsky when I met unemployed Kama Ginkas with an enormous picture under his arm. Kocherga had drawn Hamlet for him.

"What are you doing now, Varvara?" he asked.

By then I had been working in television for a couple of years, in the educational department, making programmes about botany and geography. It was there that I first got interested in directing. I look back on that period with gratitude for having learnt so much and met such wonderful people. For example, they were doing an experiment in the Botanical Gardens. For a whole month the cameras stood next to two beds of identical flowers. Each day a person walked past the first flower-bed and stuck a needle into the leaves. Then another person walked past the second flower-bed and said nice things to the flowers, such as "my darlings" or "my sweethearts". Then the first person just walked past the flower-bed, and when the flowers "saw" him they turned away, closing their leaves. But when the second person walked past, all the flowers turned their heads to watch him, as if they were smiling. Watching a film like that you can't help thinking: "Why believe in God, when Nature herself tells you that affection is repaid with affection, and evil with evil."

But when Kama Ginkas asked me to go to Krasnoyarsk (where he had been given a theatre) and play Gertrude in *Hamlet*, and said that he'd got a great crowd there, I left the television straightaway, of course. The next day I already had my ticket, popped my son Danka under my arm and got on the plane.

In Krasnoyarsk we all lived in the Circus Hotel. Each day we had to walk two kilometres to the theatre, along the walls of a silk-making factory. There was hardly anything to do in the town, so we used to spend ages in the theatre and in the hotel making up plays. It was then that I realised how much "exile" has done for our culture. Just think of Baratynsky, or Josif Brodsky, or Pushkin and Saltykov-Shchedrin or anyone you like. There's nothing to do, complete isolation, so you just write and as you write so you get peace of mind.

But I never actually played Gertrude, only rehearsed it, because there was suddenly a chance to take the play to Leningrad on tour. Kama came up to me and said: "We're going to Leningrad, Varya. Rozhin will play Claudio. Get Osipova to replace you. She won't act it as well as you do, but she looks the part more. And you can play the actress who mimes the Queen."

I couldn't help remembering the first time I went to the Theatre Institute to put my name down for an interview. "Have you ever looked at yourself in the mirror?"

Then the whole of *Hamlet* stayed in Leningrad, and I went back to Krasnoyarsk with a different, but just as great a crowd. I played Kabanikha in *The Storm* and ... directed my first production of Alexander Nikolayevich Ostrovsky's *Marriage of Balzaminov*, a favourite of mine since my student days. So I put it on and realised that it was a flop, because acting and directing are two different professions. One I had mastered, but the second I hadn't a clue about. The production was a failure for me, because I hadn't managed to do what I wanted to. There's an absolutely marvellous situation in it, when Mishenka Balzaminov, an old man, already bald, goes on dreaming about something that will never happen, which is why he is ridiculous and why his words ring out so proudly: "But I don't harm anyone by it, so just let me go on dreaming!" It was exactly our situation. The reason why I hate the rubbish they put on at the Bolshoi Drama Theatre is because they don't understand anything about this wise last play by the great Russian playwright. I thought I'd understood it, but I couldn't put the play on its feet. Still I realised that this is the secret of being a director, putting a play that has been lying on a shelf on its feet.

So I returned to my home town and went to study direction under Tovstonogov. Just before the entrance exams he saw me acting a short scene. I was playing at Zhenka Arie's, so at the interview he asked me straightaway: "What have you come here for? You're a wonderful actress."

"Then will you take me into your theatre?"

"No."

"There's your answer then."

I graduated from the Institute for the third time, and when they were handing out jobs they gave me one in Velikiye Luki. I asked them to wait an hour or two, and went to a phone to ring Tovstonogov at the theatre.

"Hello, Georgy Alexandrovich. It's Varvara Shabalina. Can I come and have a word with you? I need to discuss something."

"Allright."

So I set off for his office, feverishly composing my speech on the way, and blurted out something to the effect that I was born in St Petersburg and lived there, and had two diplomas signed by him, but now they wanted to send me off to some place called Velikiye Luki.

"As what?"

"As head producer, they said. There's a theatre there apparently."

"They've made a mistake. It's a cinema, not a theatre And what they need there is a director, not a producer, and preferably someone who's Jewish. There's nothing for you to do there."

"Then take me on as an actress. I don't need a diploma in directing at all. I really don't. You've been saying yourself all these years what a wonderful actress I am."

"But that wouldn't be right, Varvara. I've just taught you for five years!"

(That's a good one. I couldn't have seen him more than two or three times. If anyone had taught us anything it was the dear departed Katsman. God rest his soul).

He pressed a button and said: "Do we have a vacancy for the post of ordinary director? Yes? Then Varvara Borisovna Shabalina's got the job!"

Since then I've been working for twenty years in one of the leading theatres in our country, Europe and the world. I shouldn't complain because it's a job anyone else would give their eyes for, but to be quite honest all those twenty years (the best years of my life) were totally empty.

We worked a lot, and it was interesting to work with Tovstonogov and Chkheidze, and I found myself professionally, so to say. I went over to teaching direction, i.e., I didn't actually put anything on or act, but tried out parts with the actors so that when the director came along he could take what he needed for the production from everything we had tried out.

Emptiness is not determined by how busy you are nor does it actually have anything to do with that. Emptiness is what you feel when you are not being yourself. I don't know if I'm making myself clear. Perhaps it would be better to give an example.

In these twenty years so many actors and actresses have come to me for help, wanting to get out of the rut, out of the harness of being average which everyone in the theatre wears (the Bolshoi Drama Theatre included). So what happens? After two or three rehearsals that's it – they vanish into thin air. They're afraid, poor things. They don't know how to get involved in the real live theatre process, and I can't do it any other way.

Each time the story was a bit different, of course, but after a while I realised that the pattern and the "stumbling block" were always the same...

Our diploma-holding actors and actresses don't want to hear the word "mime". Ask them to act a play without the text (at a rehearsal, of course), "After all, you already know what it's about, so let's play around with the subject and perhaps that will generate something really good!" and this is what you get.

"No! We must say the words. We're dramatic actors, not mimes or ballet dancers."

"But the words are no good ..."

"Then don't use this play."

"But all words are no good!"

"What about Chekhov and Shakespeare?"

At this point I always reminded them about Gogol, how he *began by acting* each of his characters in front of the mirror and the character's words were generated by this acting.

There were masses of attempts at this, short and unsuccessful. Only on two occasions did we manage to achieve something, with Tenyakova and with Dreiden.

With Tenyakova we rehearsed Hakse's mono-play *Conversations of Frau von Stein with the absent Herr von Goethe*. We were given the play before it was officially translated.

It is interesting that at first we were always looking for props. We felt that if this or that object was not on the stage, we wouldn't be able to produce the right emotions. But then we started doing without this and that, until in the end we took away everything, having realised at last the simple and one would have thought self-evident truth that an actor needs nothing on the stage, nothing, of course, except a genuine and profound faith in what he is doing.

We made this discovery not at once, but after three months of daily rehearsals (unpaid, of course). But when nothing was left to distract attention from the acting, what pain and suffering there were in Natasha's final words: "Oh, God, why is everything so hard for all of us!"

We put this play on once or twice at the All-Russian Theatre Society, and soon afterwards the actress Tenyakova moved to Moscow. Lots of people went away from Petersburg in those days to wherever they could. But I stayed on as usual... There was no point in trying to revive the Hakse play with someone else. It was made for Natasha.

But with Seriozha Dreiden our "theatrical romance" was longer and more productive. It worked right from the start. At first we both just wanted to earn a bit extra, so we agreed to a request from the Theatre Museum to put on a couple of scenes from *The Inspector General* to illustrate the subject "Gogol and the Theatre". There were lots of actors at the first rehearsal. But after that they didn't come back. It was the same old story. They became hypnotised by the text which Seriozha and I didn't want to do. It's not often that actors get the chance to act Gogol.

I am sure that the play *Mimed Scene* was a success only because while we were rehearsing it we were always true to ourselves, and never lied to ourselves. I believe that this is the "I" that Stanislavsky was so concerned about. "I in the given circumstances". But for a long time now there have been very few people in our theatres who work on this principle. More and more it is only the "given circumstances" that are created by the hand of masters, and it never occurs to anyone to remember about the "I" today. Yet without it, without this "I", nothing can ever work on the stage.

This is why, although I go on working conscientiously at the Bolshoi Drama Theatre, I keep thinking that maybe I should go back to the Theatre Institute yet again. Only this time not to learn, but to teach. Since the good Lord has decreed that I should teach directing. Perhaps

Varvara Shabalina rehearsing with Alisa Freindlikh at the Tovstonogov Bolshoi Drama Theatre. Photo: Sergei Dreiden.

these young people could be helped in some way before they turn their "I" into some arithmetical average and learn to hide behind their professional skills!

But while this "civic exploit" (being admitted to our institute for the fourth time) is still maturing in me, I have found a way of letting off steam in television as always. I do the "One fairy tale after another" series there for the very young. After all, it's quite true what they say, that the best people in our country are the children".

* * *

In creating the *Mimed Scene* Dreiden and Shabalina were very concerned about one thing in particular, not to lie to themselves or their audience.

Finding themselves in a situation in which one actor had to act all the parts in a play, they decided that it would be foolish, to say the least, to try to do this seriously, using generally accepted forms. So a new genre appeared in this production, the genre of the rehearsal-play.

It is impossible for everything to be the main thing at rehearsals (except for dress rehearsals, that is), so in the *Mimed Scene* it was decided that some of the scenes and monologues in Gogol's play should be acted at full strength, some at half-strength, some left out completely, and some acted more than once (it was a rehearsal, after all).

So what appears before the audience is essentially "only" the intention to act Gogol's *Inspector General*, but this is precisely what makes the *Mimed Scene* so unique and impressive. Here Dreiden is as important as Gogol himself, because by submerging himself in Gogol's text, the actor is taking the audience into the holy of holies, one of the greatest mysteries in the world, the creative process: the process of the mastering and interpreting by one person, the actor, of the creative intent of another person, the playwright.

Dreiden opens the production by coming on stage in the ordinary sort of clothes that actors usually come to rehearsals in (you remember his light-coloured shirt and jumper, because after a while, when he gets into a rage, he pulls his jumper off). He is holding a small book, Gogol's play *The Inspector General*. He carefully reads out the description of the famous final "mimed scene", trying to adapt himself to each of the many characters in it: the Mayor – "with arms outstretched and head thrown back" (stretches out his arms and throws back his head); the two Skvoznik-Dmukhanovskaya women – "their whole body straining towards him with every moment" (tries to strain his "whole body", but doesn't succeed at once, particularly as he has only one body, but Gogol is talking about two); Luka Lukich, "who is innocently confused" (squats down, as if hiding away in a corner, and surveys the audience from there, trying to demonstrate his innocence of what has taken place). There are also the ladies "with a most satirical expression on their faces", and Korobkin, and so on. And each of these characters does not start off behind the scenes so as to come on stage "nice and ready", but appears in front of us, armed not with a costume, make-up and other theatrical appurtenances, but solely with the power of his actor's imagination embodied in his acting.

One of the elements that ensured the success of Dreiden's bold enterprise, was undoubtedly the fact that Gogol's text about the panic and confusion caused in a small provincial town by the arrival of a minor official, who is mistaken for a very important person, an inspector general, is something that every member of a Russian audience has known since childhood. And it is this knowledge of the play by the audience that enables the actor to play around with the "Gogolian basis" in all sorts of ways. Not only does Dreiden never act the text of the *Inspector General* consecutively and in full, but he also occasionally adds his own speeches. True, this is not at all the same as "going off on your own" when an actor forgets about the author's text and says anything that comes into his head.

Dreiden preserves unchanged the lines of Gogol's characters. The new lines invented by Dreiden himself record the "inner monologue" which is for every actor the "springboard" from which he dives into the playwright's text. An actor usually keeps this "inner monologue" to himself, concealing it from the audience. Dreiden does the reverse, by sharing his own utterances with the audience. In this particular case the "hybrid" of different styles (the 19th century and the present day) has the amazing effect of enabling the audience to see straightaway that the customs and events portrayed in Gogol's comedy are still highly relevant today.

Dreiden also expounds aloud and in his own words the torment which the actor experiences in the process of mastering a new role. In this case he talks to the audience as if they were colleagues faced with the same task as he is, of understanding and acting Gogol's characters, finding the key to interpreting them. Thus, leaving for a while outside his and our attention the development of the different lines in the plot, he turns to the audience with roughly the following words:

"The Mayor... The Mayor... How should he be acted? He should really spend his time looking after the town. Yes, I see. That's like I should spend my time making sure that the audience finds it interesting. But he doesn't do his work, the scoundrel, he plays his part badly and spends his time on quite different things."

And, immersing himself mentally in the Mayor, the actor shows us with lethal irony in a short mime precisely how the Mayor demonstrates to those around him his concern for the townspeople, while all the time he is hoping that they will all suddenly die of the plague or, if the worst comes to the worst, the devil take them!

The most impressive "digressions" from Gogol in Dreiden's performance are when he gets to Khlestakov, particularly the famous scene when he lies. It must be said here that the actor possesses a remarkable talent for literary mystification, because his fantasies (or rather Khlestakov's) are completely in the same vein as those of Nikolai Vassilievich. What is more the degree of grotesque depends with him on two things: the specific audience and the specific historical moment. Here, of course, it must be emphasised that, like Gogol, Dreiden never has recourse to direct political allusions and avoids obvious civic pathos and other superficial devices which help one win cheap authority with the public.

Dreiden is just over fifty, and that is the wonderful age when a person still possesses enough strength and energy, but already feels the constant inner need to interpret life as such. And Gogol is par excellence one of those authors who make it possible to do this. So this is why, in the middle of acting Luka Lukich "...if anybody even one rank higher starts talking to me, I get in such a tizzy...", Dreiden suddenly stops and expresses amazement at just how low a person can get, doing so not in words, but simply by shaking off the mask of this "hero", like you might shake mud off a coat. This he picks up this "mud" and looks at it for a long time, pityingly.

Dreiden is one of those actors who have mastered the Stanislavsky method and the ideas of Brecht's epic theatre. He does not set emotion against alienation, but makes skilful use of both, combining them organically in his acting.

But the main thing here lies not in the methods, nor in Gogol's play from which Dreiden tries to digress all the time. The main thing is that for the whole evening the audience comes into close contact with a person who has thought and suffered a great deal, but not lost his sense of humour.

For some reason I can easily imagine an episode in the production *Mimed Scene* which has never appeared in it, but could easily arise if Dreiden finds out that I am writing about him for the Russian Archive publishers. Khlestakov's monologue would contain something like the following tirade: "... and I wrote Zagoskin's works as well. Or take this example. There's Markova, a theatre critic, who won't let you lie. A most amusing event took place today. Sir Robert Robertson arrived in St Petersburg from England, and kept insisting that she should write about Dreiden, about Khlestakov, that is, i.e., about Dreiden (what difference does it make anyway). Although she's a well-known critic and has written a book about Marcel Marceau, when it comes to me she says: "No, Sir Robertson, I can't. Dreiden's whole performance is improvisation, which can't be written down. However hard I tried, the English would never be able to understand anything."

So they both rushed over to me. And I wrote it for them, of course. So now I'll have to go to England, or who will translate it for them.

I can just imagine how the audience would burst out laughing after that, remembering all the numerous stories connected with the mass, frenzied desire of Russians today to have foreign contacts and organise joint ventures with foreign partners. But Dreiden in the form of Khlestakov goes on "lying", so glibly that it sounds very like the truth. Particularly as it really is impossible to describe the *Mimed Scene*. For he acts it differently each time, which demands extreme mobilisation from the actor and gives the audience the richly rewarding contact which is the theatre's raison d'etre.

But as for the English not understanding, that's a joke, of course. The English did understand, and so did the Germans, and the Americans, and the French, because the *Mimed Scene* has been shown at many international festivals.

In St Petersburg it is only put on two or three times a month for the simple reason that it takes time to prepare yourself properly to act the play in a new way all over again.

A youth rehabilitation centre

The Subbota (Saturday) theatre-club, popular with young Leningraders, was already thinking about how to celebrate its tenth anniversary, but the Young Communist magazine was still openly sceptical. "... The founder members of Leningrad's Subbota theatre-club like to think that their first meeting was pure chance. Someone was giving a lecture on the history of the theatre in one of the district palaces of culture. A group of young people wandered in to listen – they had been singing to a guitar in a nearby backyard, until the piercing Baltic wind had driven them to seek shelter. Something in the lecture interested them. / ... / You can surely only link the setting up of an enterprising youth club with a sudden shower of rain for the sake of a nice club legend" (Young Communist, 1976, No. 6).

In 1994 the Subbota theatre-club, that veteran of the studio movement, celebrated its twenty-fifth birthday. Since it was set up a great deal has changed in the life of the country and in the minds of its people (the Young Communist magazine is no longer with us, for example). The troupe at Subbota has changed several times. Perhaps the only person who remains is its director, Yuri Alexandrovich Smirnov-Nesvitsky. At first they did not have a definite programme, and the level of knowledge and culture of the first troupe was not very high. They lacked a great deal, but they themselves suffered only from the fact that they had no one to confide in, they were not integrated, or, as modern psychology would say, they lacked a referential group.

In his book *One More Life* about Subbota's first ten years Yuri Smirnov-Nesvitsky recalls the moment when the theatre-club was born. It was "something like this: everyone has their own dream, their own ideal theatre. But one person doesn't make a theatre. So several people got together, smiled at one another ... and in the stillness there arose an eternal friendship – a theatre."

In other words, their theatre-club began with casual contact, but with time it began to preach a form of "theatralised communication". United "in a circle", they learned to be honest with one another. And that was all! But it turned out to be quite enough not only to bring them together, but to attract crowds of people who marvelled at their art of finding themselves, their wonderful ability to be honest. The honesty of the "Subbotans" enabled audiences to learn at first hand about the dramatic conflicts in the life of a whole generation.

The main principle and, if one can put it like this, "artistic image" which formed the basis of the first public performance (the production *Theatre Pages*) was the chain.

The concept of the "chain" was sickeningly familiar to any Soviet person in those days. It was something you knew about from kindergarten, when all the children had to hold on to a long piece of rope with one hand when they went out for a walk, and not let go of it. With age these controlling fetters became increasingly restrictive, although less obvious. In the 1980s young rock musicians wrote a popular song about this, which was actually called "Fettered by a single chain" (meaning the whole Soviet people).

Unexpectedly for many members of the audience the concept of the chain acquired its original sense of unity and solidarity in Subbota. Joining hands firmly, so as not to be pulled apart, the Subbotans walked round the stage at the same pace, chanting a song, reciting a poem, or uttering monologues addressed to the audience. They did not make the slightest effort to be actors. On the contrary, they did everything for themselves alone. None of them was made up, and they were dressed in their own clothes, their best clothes incidentally.

The Visitors' Book which they have kept here since the very first day contains the following entry about this performance: "A group of young people, all holding hands. Talking and singing. And their eyes! Who are they? They understand each other at the slightest gesture, the slightest word. What a wonderful world! I sat in the first row and wept. And I didn't feel ashamed. I shall now go down on my knees and beg them for a piece of friendship. It's called a chain. It's happiness."

"*Theatre Pages*", Yuri Alexandrovich recalls. "was like the tiny pieces of glass that slide around in a kaleidoscope. The episodes fitted into the general mood. And it was this mood, not a definite subject, that held the performance together."

Already in *Theatre Pages* the main features of all Subbota's subsequent productions could be seen. And the most important one was that when they came on to the stage they played themselves and not someone else. They actually played, and in so doing achieved the degree of revelation in everyday situations which they wanted. The path to themselves lay through mastering the equation "the role = me".

As a result the dramatic foundation had to be entirely unusual, created out of themselves, generated from the stillness which preceded the confessional mood.

Smirnov-Nesvitsky recalls: "After we had formed a circle, we sat together in complete silence. The silence itself generated completely new sensations. In the silence you can sense the mood of the person next to you, the general mood shared by everyone. Your imagination starts working, you feel the urge to confess, you want to talk. This organic silence can act as a device for creating a play-talk.

The source of our first scenario was the general mood which arose from this organic silence, then from the confessions in the silence and, finally, from songs. Both then and later songs played an important part in Subbota productions. We composed them ourselves and took them from life. An amateur actor cannot always master a complex psychological state, but he can convey a similar state in a character through a song. This has been proved time and time again by the traditions of folk creativity."

The solid core of Subbota has always been made up mainly of eighteen-year-olds, the age when you feel a particularly strong need to assert yourself, by getting to know yourself and comparing yourself with the world around you. This whole complex of highly complicated emotions they called "existing from yourself".

By the time of their next production *Teenage Party* their principles of work were still the same, but the result was different and also about something different, because by then the joy of getting to know one another had given way to more complex relationships between the Subbotans themselves. As is usually the case, various likes and dislikes developed within the collective and the occasional clash arose from time to time. And since the most valuable thing about the Subbotans had always been their honesty, they told the audience outright in this new production about all the problems they were experiencing. The effect was quite unexpected: behind these individual examples it was easy to detect architypal models in which members of the audience recognised themselves. After all everyone had experienced first love, hurt pride, etc. at some time or other.

The public nature of this confession had the very powerful effect of assisting the development of everyone who took part in and helped to create the production.

In a way the whole business reminded one of the well-known and now popular method of group psychotherapy, which is used to treat neurosis, the disease of unsolved problems. But at the beginning of the seventies these para-theatrical forms were not only not cultivated in our country, but were tacitly banned, a ban which Subbota equally tacitly (and perhaps unexpectedly for itself) ignored.

After the first night of *Teenage Party* it became quite clear that the Subbota theatre-club was focusing its attention primarily on young people's communication problems. Yet the way in which these problems were studied here immediately attracted not only members of the then large and young underground, but also well-known intellectuals, scientists, writers and theatre critics, the flower of the intelligentsia, so to say, and not only Leningraders either.

In those years the adaptation of young people to their social environment was a really painful process with pretty dismal prospects.

Subbota knew all about this, not from hearsay, but from personal experience. But they were not going to let it get them down. Their productions often attracted people full of reckless youthful energy and fond of indulging in endless practical jokes, uninhibited by the rules of real everyday life.

It was against this background that another distinguishing feature of the artistic structure of Subbota's productions appeared, the use of masks. For example, Manya Oshibkina, a teenager who is always making mistakes ("oshibki" in Russian), i.e., falling for the wrong guy. Or the Ikarus bus mask, that is, a blinkered person who is capable of moving around in life in straight lines only (at that time the city has just been inundated with these clumsy, slow-moving buses, so the name of the mask was very topical). Another popular mask was that of the mongrel stray Fifi Dog. The associations here covered a whole range of emotions from strong sense of affection to the constant torment caused by an inferiority complex.

Finally came a production which synthesised everything that had been achieved up to then. It was called "The Theatricalised Circle" and was conceived and produced as a talk-play with the audience.

Already in the foyer the theatre staff asked everyone as they came in "Are you a go-getter or a stick-in-the-mud?" and gave them corresponding badges – a smiling face for the go-getters and a miserable face for the stick-in-the-muds. The former were shown to seats at the front and the latter at the back. The unusual aim of the production was to ensure active audience participation in what was happening on the stage. The Subbotans invited members of the audience to come up and dance, sing, chat about young people's problems and difficulties, and take part in all sorts of practical jokes. What made it work was the fact that they were all the same age and shared the same interests. The Subbotans made no attempt to parade in front of their fellow-teenagers as toffee-nosed servants of the muses. On the contrary, they behaved very democratically, not hiding their merits or their faults. The habit of being honest was by now so deeply engrained that they felt they could create a play-reflection on the fate of a whole generation, the generation that was later to be called "superfluous", the generation whose hopes, dreams and energy had been crushed by the insuperable obstacles that surrounded everyone in the so-called "age of stagnation". What they talked about here was not so much politics as something much bigger, the atmosphere of everyday life, the spiritual "ecology" that had been so relentlessly polluted and destroyed by politics.

As usual the characters in the next production entitled *Windows, Streets, Backyards* were not exceptional people, but ordinary teenagers from the courtyards. But the simpler their wishes, the more tragic the sense that these wishes could never be fulfilled. What could be more harmless than wanting to have a dog? Seventeen-year-old Nina has been longing for a pedigree dog for years, but then a mongrel turns up (one of the versions of the Fifi mask, so a very human-looking "dog"). They get so fond of each other that they become inseparable. The audience has witnessed (and therefore to some extent participated in) this process which had its problems. Then one day the dog disappears. Some boys have tortured it to death. They are not portrayed as villains in the play, but rather as kids who do not know where to turn, like the dog itself and its owner at one stage.

"It's all so hard and all so simple". This line from one of the songs in which *Windows, Streets, Backyards* abounded, like earlier productions, became its leitmotif. Songs alternated with the short sketches that made up the scenario, which was written by the performers themselves (not without the assistance of an artistic director, of course).

Once found, the basic scheme of the Subbotan productions remained practically unchanged, yet new productions never repeated old ones. The secret of this was very simple: roughly every five years the Subbota troupe changed and a new generation came into the theatre, as it did into the world … with its own problems, its own assumptions and values. So Subbota productions, in spite of the unchanging principles that underlay them, were always in touch with the times and never the same. Here is just one example of this. Although not a theatre obsessed with political intrigue, it was Subbota that only a year before the August putsch of 1991 put on *Macbeth* which conveyed very accurately the atmosphere of chaos accompanied by the struggle for power that was just beginning in our country.

In *Edinstvo (Unity)*, one of the new newspapers (of which there were so many at that time), O. Zavyalova published a review of *Macbeth* under the title "Childish dreams of the age of perestroika", which showed clearly how much the mood and hopes of the Subbotans had changed compared with what they were at the beginning:

CHILDISH DREAMS OF THE AGE OF PERESTROIKA

Theatre news: the Subbota theatre-club has put on *Macbeth*. The production is extremely polemical and very avant garde. One is even afraid to describe it. Lovers of the classics and purity of style can throw stones. In its defence it must be said: yes, the witches here do have a blood test for AIDS and Macbeth and his lady do rush around the stage from time to time in their birthday suits. Yes, some of the characters are standing for people's deputies and the Globe theatre troupe is riven by intrigue, while

Shakespeare's blood-covered sergeant becomes one of the main heroes and is dressed in the green spotted uniform of an international soldier.

I can just imagine Shakespeare's enormous shadow looming over the theatre studio's tiny stage. But he can sleep peacefully, I assure you. Nor should our scholars, docents and candidates of science worry unduly. Smirnov-Nesvitsky, the author and director of this scenic composition, warns us clearly on the poster: "based on motifs..." The super-freedom of the treatment, I make so bold to say, was necessary not in order to dance on the remnants of the great tragedy. By plunging into the sphere of form, the theatre-studio does not in fact stray very far from Shakespeare. At any rate no further than the academic theatres who put him on respectably and boringly, although closer to the text.

In this composition "based on motifs" the main motif of the tragedy is elaborated with respect and understanding. The world intrigue of evil, the satanic struggle for power (acted out on all levels, from political skirmishes to theatre intrigue) – this is the mainspring of the spectacle which destroys everything, sparing no one and executing victims and butchers alike, guilty and innocent. Subbota has arranged the old and terrible melody in super-modern rock rhythms, and the whole fabric of the production is incredibly relevant and familiar.

The refrain "O, theatre of non-residential accommodation!" runs through the play. And the accommodation really is non-residential. On the stage we see a rusty bedstead, a peeling park bench and an iron cage the height of a man, the sort of cage one might find standing empty in a super-market these days (they used to have food in them). A rubbish dump, alias our ecological niche. The beams hang menacingly overhead, something is dripping from the ceiling and the plumber just doesn't want to know. Everything is on the verge of collapse. A dress rehearsal for the apocalypse. And a frayed and patched curtain. The curtain of a "burnt-out theatre".

The production is called "Who's that covered in blood". Not only the sergeant is blood-covered. A witch who looks like a rock star is rushing round the stage with a bowl of blood – there's plenty for everyone. "Who's that covered in blood" wouldn't be a bad name for the TV programme "600 seconds", would it? The aesthetics of this production are quite close to Alexander Nevzorov's kaleidoscope of city news that appears each evening on Petersburg television. The same frenzied rush of "bloody" shots, the same poverty-stricken life verging on collapse and the absurd. Only whereas Nevzorov is not joking as a rule, this is Subbota's sole salvation, its very foundation. And whereas Nevzorov tries to scare you with subjects from other people's "sordid" lives, Subbota admits sadly through Banquo's lips: we are all homeless and share the same fate.

An ordinary day's work at Subbota.

Against the background of the politicised art of recent years this production impresses one as being extremely de-ideologised. All the fearful and funny, familiar and strange "birthmarks" of the present day are demonstrated here but not with passionate denunciation. All the facts of life – AIDS, the impassioned parliamentary battles, the boys from Afghanistan "with their bloodshot eyes" – all this is acted through the prism of a modern young person's mind, whose poor head is dazed by the picture of the world that oppresses it.

If I had to define the genre of this work (which is almost impossible because it keeps floating away), I would call what takes place on the stage a Russian folk dream. It is a mixture of reality and premonition, our fears and our pain, our liberating black humour ("save yourself if you can!" and our all-embracing senility which, as we know, tends to progress.

This split personality, riven by a stream of TV, audio, printed, street and so on information, this underground voice is one of the main heroes in the production. It is not mentioned on the poster, but is clearly present on the stage. As for the other characters, I would prefer not to pick out anyone in particular. It is a collective work and the whole team acts in it ("team thinking," as they say in football). Yet two stars do shine out very clearly, to my mind. They are K. Destilyator's Lady Macbeth (with her fantastic entrance to the rock hit "Alain Delon don't drink eau-de-cologne!") She strides down the theatre steps triumphantly and impressively, like a first lady walking down a plane ramp. And the fourth witch, who does not exist in Shakespeare's play, but was invented by the theatre and is played by M. Veselova. This ginger-headed singer with the chalk white face and wonderful husky voice, an "untaught" heroine, performs her part with polished brilliance and charm.

I couldn't help thinking that if the theatre is able to play these unchildish games, get such pleasure from it and convey that pleasure to the audience, it must mean that all is not lost. For what is this crazy spectacle if not the overcoming of life by acting, when humour and artistry rescue the mind from mounting nightmares and light up the shaking world through the crystal of irony. The theme of the theatre, of acting and overcoming shines throughout the play like a torch, relieving the darkness. And when things become quite intolerable, the Subbota theatre troupe assembles behind the torn curtain, in other words, the Globe theatre company, the villains and angels all join together, and the theatre's First Lady recites like a prayer: "Oh, theatre of non-residential accommodation! You are alone in the total darkness! And if one solitary last spectator comes to us, we shall play before him..." A guitar drowns the shouting, screams and clamouring voices for a while and the bedlam recedes...

Watching this production is like turning the knobs of a radio. First the long waves, then the medium waves and then the short waves. You can hear the sound of voices, intonations, a delusion of sounds, gnashing of teeth, languages, melodies, explosions and silence... Sometimes the fabric of the production seems so tattered that one more tug and that will be the end of it. It will split into pieces from the tension, the confusion of meanings, hints, and parodies. But no, it still hangs together. I suspect that this "splintering" is not a mistake in the blueprints or a flaw in the performance, but a structural principle. The production "Who's that covered in blood" does not strive to be integrated and well-balanced, just as the mass consciousness cannot be integrated and well-balanced. What is more, it does not strive to be finished! It is an absolutely open-ended structure. The theatrical text is not wedded to the space of the stage for now and ever more. So if during a performance Matthias Rust suddenly lands on the stage, or Maradona runs out with a football, or Yegor Kuzmich Ligachev suddenly makes an election speech, Subbota continues without batting an eyelid. Taking the new circumstances into account.

* * *

It can be said without exaggeration that the Subbota Theatre team have always acted "for themselves", put on plays proceeding from themselves and tried to realise themselves, which means, finding themselves.

During the 25th-anniversary celebrations of Subbota, a lot of people recalled that the theatre-club had started "just like that", just because a group of teenagers singing their simple home-made songs to a guitar in a backyard had nowhere to go when it started raining and went into the nearest house of culture to get warm. And on that particular evening Dr. Yuri Alexandrovich Smirnov-Nesvitsky, a serious-minded and well-respected person, eminent scholar, author of many definitive studies on the Soviet theatre, member of the Union of Writers and Union of Theatre Workers, who worked for many years in one of the world's oldest institutes for research into the arts, which is next to St Isaac's Cathedral in one of St Petersburg's loveliest squares, was giving a lecture on the work of Evgeny Bagrationovich Vakhtangov, the legendary producer who succeeded, although mortally ill and in the bitterly hard years of the Civil War, in creating the most sparkling and delightful production in the whole history of the Russian theatre, *Princess Turandot* based on the story by Carlo Gozzi.

That evening "a certain something" attracted the interest of the teenagers from the backyard and ever since then our city has had the Subbota theatre-club, Subbota (Saturday) being the day when a person can escape from the oppressive tedium of ordinary weekdays and find his ideal self.

P.S. Today Subbota is so well-known that the Mayor's Office of St Petersburg has found it possible to grant this collective the status of a municipal state theatre.

Permanent premises for Subbota are now being built in the city centre (in the reconstructed complex of the Apraxin Court).

Let's hope to goodness that as a result of these changes Subbota won't turn into an ordinary weekday.

No theatre company can survive today without substantial grants, but what state patronage does to theatres we have seen not so long ago.

An ecological niche

Most theatre studios which announced their existence in the 1980s with the advent of the age of glasnost' had by then traversed the thorny path of amateur love of the theatre for many years. This path can be called thorny if only for the fact that these studios faced the constant threat of a tragic "lethal end", the risk of simply being extinguished, in spite of all their efforts and hard work. This risk was and still is absolutely real.

In the age of stagnation this involved, first and foremost, ideological bans. Today, in the age of cardinal change and destruction, it is lack of funds.

And yet they still exist, so it is important to understand the nature of their enviable stamina. This is determined, as a rule, by sociocultural principles which to some extent remind one of those found earlier in the "hippies". Only the "theatre rebels" are protesting not against civilisation as such, but against the existing forms and norms of theatre culture. Which is why they seek refuge not in "field and forests", but in what we might call the "non-theatre space" of cities. For the most part this means cellars, semi-basements and attics, i.e., what is usually referred to as "non-residential accommodation" in Russia.

They also remind us of the hippies, because the life of theatre-studio people is organised like that of the commune, which, incidentally, includes their fairly numerous admirers. All this, of course, creates a special atmosphere at their productions and compels us to study not only the results of their work, but also the vital process that accompanies this work and is an integral part of their creativity.

* * *

In the tiny auditorium of the Theatre of the Rain, which holds about 150, it is always stuffy, and also damp and dank at the same time. The age-old Petersburg chill gets right into your bones here. Yet twice a week (on Saturdays and Sundays which is when performances are given here) the hall is absolutely packed.

One review of a Theatre of the Rain production began like this: "I always feel scared and bitter in old Petersburg courtyards. The grey, relentlessly identical walls, the bleak, dusty windows ... I cannot look the children in the yards in the eye – no, their eyes are not adult, serious or sad – they are old before their time and without hope, on pale, dirty faces.

These yards are a heart-breaking but essential prelude to what I want to talk about ..."

The Theatre of the Rain. Photo: Irina Kuzmina.

A sense of poignant despair is something very familiar to the creators of the Theatre of the Rain, which is located in the semi-basement of one of these courtyards.

Only you would certainly not say that these young people's eyes are without hope, unless you remarked that they shine with "hopeless" idealism, which, like a good cocktail, is a mixture of daring, goodwill and infectious youth laced with a fair portion of self-irony, however.

This probably explains why their favourite playwright is Chekhov, and his *Three Sisters* the theatre's number one play.

It was with Chekhov's *Seagull* that Natasha Nikitina, the team's leader, began her career as a director. And it was in the process of rehearsing *The Seagull* that the Theatre of the Rain was born, although at that moment all the people taking part in it were still Subbotans. The appearance of their own production enabled them to break away from the Subbota theatre-club and embark on a voyage of their own.

This reproduction of amateur studios by gemmation is a fairly ordinary, even logical, occurrence. In a way the theatre (the amateur theatre in particular) is like a family. And in a family the grown-up children always strive to break away from their parents.

Natasha Nikitina had this to say about herself and how her circle of friends grew up:

"I first started thinking seriously about the theatre when I saw some diploma productions by the famous Tovstonogov course, which were put on as *Visible Song* and *West Side Story*. These productions shook me to the core. They were unlike everything that was vegetating around. The productions by the Tovstonogians were full of the youth and imagination of those who created and performed them. I saw each of them about ten times. After that the Lenkom, which had taken them in, became like home to me. And the actors like members of my family, although I didn't know any of them personally.

By the time I left school I had decided to try for the Theatre Institute, the acting faculty, of course (I didn't have even the vaguest idea that any other faculties existed).

But my mother and father told me outright: "If you go to the Theatre Institute, you're no daughter of ours, because the theatre is not a profession that can guarantee you a decent wage, and the sort of people who take it up are idle layabouts, they don't produce anything."

My timid remarks that the theatre produces precious and essential sustenance for the soul were dismissed out of hand. Neither then nor now has there ever been any agreement in our family on personal or so-called socio-political questions. For example, I voted for Yeltsin and my parents voted against him, particularly my father. He is an absolutely honest man, an excellent specialist (a geodesist) and a convinced communist.

All his life he has believed in these ideals and now that they have collapsed he has become physically ill, because he can no longer understand what is happening around him and how he can go on living.

I feel very sorry for him, but I am different. However, on that occasion my father succeeded in breaking me, or rather, in undermining my albeit slight confidence in myself. So I went to LITMO (the Leningrad Institute of Precision Mechanics and Optics) instead. The reason for this choice was simply that the institute was the nearest establishment of higher education to my beloved Leninsky Komsomol Theatre.

I was reconciled to the idea of a technical education by the fact that Senya Spivak, one of the founders of Subbota, worked at LITMO. He is now head director of the Molodezhny Theatre, but at that time he was still studying direction at the Theatre Institute.

He used to put on special faculty evenings at our Institute, thanks to which we could express ourselves in public. It was a special sort of language, of course, a kind of Aesopian one, but the audience which consisted of fellow students, understood us at the drop of a hat.

It was Senya Spivak who took me to Subbota, where everyone was as crazy about the theatre as I was. And just as unable to adapt themselves to the life around them as I was too. In the company of like-minded people, I began to have faith in myself. So much so that in the winter I left LITMO, just before my final year, with the firm intention of applying in six months time for the direction faculty of the Institute of Culture, which trained people for amateur theatres (I wasn't attracted to the state ones, they were changing quickly and not for the best. Let's put it like this, they worked, but they did not create anything).

By then I had begun to sort out what was what in theatre professions. I was now more attracted by directing than anything else. As far as acting was concerned, I hadn't exactly gone off it, but... Firstly, I now realised that my appearance would type-cast me for the role of standard heroines only, which meant a lots of my favourite parts, but the main thing was (although this is secondly), that I turned out to have a "commanding" sort of character. I had a natural urge to be a leader.

There was a terrible outcry in LITMO when I said I was leaving. I used to get top marks for everything, there was a photograph of me on the board of honour as a very socially conscious and active student, I was a member of the institute's young communist branch, the head of a building team, and so on and so forth.

Everyone told me I was a fool. "If you don't like your profession you can always join the party and make party work your career instead. You're a wonderful organiser, you'll live in clover!"

But, goodness me, how happy I am that I acted as my intuition told me, that is, refused to join the party and live in clover.

After that I used to "disappear" to Subbota every evening, and in the daytime I worked at the Institute of Culture (as a secretary in the dean's office). But I didn't go and study there, because next spring my daughter was born. And then I realised for the first time exactly how dependent any Soviet woman who allows herself the luxury of having a child becomes on all and sundry.

My mother, who was perfectly familiar with this special feature of Soviet life, understood the situation perfectly and issued me with a new ultimatum: "If you go and study directing, you can look after the child yourself, but if you go back to LITMO, we'll look after it until you finish."

I went back to LITMO, not for the sake of getting a computer specialist diploma, but because I remembered there was lots of theatre work there. LITMO was also deciphered as a joke by analogy with the Leningrad Institute of the Theatre, Music and Cinematography (LTITMiK in Russian). Students also used to joke that our institute stood for the Leningrad Institute of the Theatre, Music and Opportunism (LITMO). Actually, as I found out later, LITMO was not the only technical higher educational establishment with a strong interest in the arts.

I had found another safety-valve, so life again acquired meaning. The only worrying thing was that according to the regulations each young specialist after graduating had to spend three years working wherever the state sent him or her in return for receiving an education. This was called the "vyshka", an abbreviation for capital punishment.

I kept getting top marks as before, and the dean persuaded me to agree to a compromise. I would work for a year only where I was sent and after that I would either get a "free diploma" or do post-graduate research.

That year was the most nightmarish in my life, although outwardly the most prosperous. Twice a month I received my pay on which I could live perfectly well, but for this I had to sit in my place and do nothing each day for eight hours twelve minutes. There were about thirty people in our laboratory at a high-security design bureau, and only two or three of them actually did any research, thinking up a subject and a plan of work. The rest, mostly women, spent the time knitting, reading books and listening happily to my stories about the theatre and some recent first nights.

Only when the boss came into the room did everything grab a pencil feverishly and start chewing the end nervously, head in hand. Which is how the process of intense creative thought was traditionally depicted.

All these games were enough to make a normal person go round the bend.

In the end I decided to use the time to get some sleep, because each day after work I rushed over to Subbota and stayed there late (sometimes until after midnight).

At the end of the year I was at last free of this "non-life" and went to work in Subbota. They paid me forty roubles a month there at first, then eighty, which was still much less than at my first job, but I would have agreed to work there for nothing.

It was 1982. Not long before this the "older generation" had left Subbota en masse, which happens every four or five years. The depleted repertoire had to be revived quickly. I knew these plays by heart, of course, and the remaining actors too. So the work was easy and informal. We did not simply copy the old version, but created a new one.

A whole series of revivals of old plays followed, such as *Saturdays, Five Corners* (1982), *The Theatricalised Circle* (1983), *The Burden of Human Passions* (1984) and *Windows, Streets, Backyards* (1987). Apart from revivals I also put on my own productions at Subbota. In 1986 I directed *The Seagull*, in 1987 I did *Theatre Pages* with some beginners and in 1988 *Swift*.

And then … Then the next mass exodus from Subbota took place. And this time it was my turn. About half the troupe followed me. After a highly unpleased general meeting, we found ourselves outside in the pouring rain… We had nothing but ourselves, but inside us were our productions, past and future."

* * *

The breaking away process ended with self-determination and the first night of *Three Sisters* based on Chekhov.

Space is very "cramped" in this production. But not just because the stage at the Theatre of the Rain is a small one. The "crampedness" is one of the central themes here: the characters have nowhere to go both literally and figuratively.

Throughout the play all the characters taking part in it are on stage almost all the time. They share the same, very constricted "life space", which reminds one albeit very remotely (mainly in terms of atmosphere rather than form) of the sense of vulnerability so familiar to the inhabitants of Leningrad's numerous communal flats.

In spite of Chekhov's stage directions the sets for this space are always the same: the small circle of the stage, which becomes in turn the rooms in the Prozorovs' house, and the garden, and in fact the "life space" of each of these people. There is a tree next to the piano, and the garden bench is used sometimes as a garden bench and sometimes as a sofa in a study, although the tree is always there. There are actually a lot of trees, but they are all bare (without a single leaf or even twig),

Scene from the Theatre of the Rain's *Three Sisters*, based on Chekhov's play.
Photo: Irina Kuzmina.

with sawn-off tops. They are dying, almost dead, and only the skeleton
remains to remind one of their earlier blossoming.

Against the background of this non-being you sense all the more
strongly that the characters in Chekhov's drama are all incredibly young:
all of them, from Irina to the nurse who looked after the sisters' mother,

Chebutykin who has only a year to go to his pension and Ferapont, whom age made hard of hearing long ago.

There are no elderly actors in the Theatre of the Rain, only young ones. But the reason is not this difference in age. They deliberately do not use make-up or any of the other devices with the help of which old age is usually depicted in the theatre (a shuffling gait, mumbling speech, etc.). In each of Chekhov's characters the actors have managed to find the "child", who, as we know, is somewhere deep down in each of us. This basic human feature, which adults usually conceal or suppress in themselves, is materialised, presented to the audience visually, in the Theatre of the Rain production. The characters here are not only young in appearance. They are also very spontaneous in their emotional outpourings, like children.

Tusenbach, for example, exclaims happily, almost rapturously: "Yes, I am ugly!" While Irina, beautiful, radiant Irina, quite oblivious of herself and others, curses her work at the telegraph office, because it gives her nothing but exhaustion. "Old" Dr Chebutykin takes advantage of any excuse to pull funny faces. Olga does not like the part of the eldest sister, headmistress and person in charge of the household. She keeps trying to join in her sisters' frivolities. But the more she attempts to throw off her endless duties, the more demands they make upon her. You can't help feeling sorry for Soleny with his awful chip on his shoulder. He resembles a poor waif who is aggressive because he is so defenceless.

To some extent or other all the characters in the play are young at heart – still at the delightful stage when a person is sure that his real life will begin tomorrow, the stage when he lives in a dream, absorbed in it and therefore happy.

The most terrible thing for all these people is time, which, as we know, goes on and on, never stopping, and which is relentless if only for the fact that it carries away even the most precious dreams. And this is all the more tragic if the dreams have not been realised, because with time even the brightest hopes fade and can no longer give joy to anyone, even their owner.

The action in Chekhov's play ends in autumn, when life must die down in both the countryside and the town (as the soldiers leave) and the birds fly off to warmer climes.

When the soldiers have finally disappeared and their music has fallen silent, melting into the distance, you hear the sound of migrating birds and the sisters turn their faces up to the sky. And "suddenly it's as if wings had grown" (as Irina has just said) on the sisters. Spreading out their arms and gazing at the horizon, Olga, Masha and Irina begin slowly (painfully slowly) to imitate the movements of birds.

And gradually all the other characters in Chekhov's play (and perhaps not only Chekhov's) join them, a flock, forming the traditional v-shape of migrating cranes.

This imitation flight lasts for a long time, so long that you begin to think they really are flying. But then the attraction of the earth becomes ever stronger and the movement of their wings weaker, until these people are kneeling on the ground with their hands raised to the heavens in supplication and their figures fade into dim outlines which are gradually swallowed up by the approaching darkness.

And only the music plays on.

* * *

In order to get the right to own the semi-basement premises at number 130 on the embankment of the Fontanka River, the Theatre of the Rain first had to find out about the new regulations (or rather lack of them) introduced by that time in our country, where a naked and unforgiveable struggle for power had begun. True, the most effective help was the assistance which individual people gave just for the sake of it, i.e., gratis, out of the goodness of their hearts, as has been the custom in Russia since very early times.

They converted and equipped the premises themselves. No one gave them any sizeable grants for this purpose, of course. Some things were brought from home, others were found on rubbish tips. And wooden boards, for example, were "secretly borrowed" from a long-term building project site. They even made use of rods from the crates which are used here to carry empty wine and spirits bottles and then usually dumped not far from the shop where the bottles have been delivered.

On one occasion some of the actors found themselves in the police-station for such exploits. You can imagine their surprise when those custodians of the peace actually sympathised with their problems and decided to let them go home.

By fair means or foul the stage and auditorium, an amphitheatre seating 56, were eventually built, even a cloakroom by the entrance (in a hole one-and-a-half metres deep).

Later, when the Theatre of the Rain had acquired not only its own premises, but also a repertoire (with revivals of *The Seagull* and *Swift* and new productions of *The Three Sisters*, *The Rain Seller* and *Giddup* based on the play by Nina Sadur) sponsors suddenly began to appear. Unfortunately, they tended to disappear just as quickly and unexpectedly. Private business is still a rather precarious occupation in Russia, and being a patron is an even more thankless task.

And so it happened that from the very start the Theatre of the Rain actors were not paid for months on end. And no matter what how big their income was, some of it always went to pay the other staff, the scene shifters, light and sound technicians and cleaners. If they want to have the chance to do something creative the actors have to take on another job to earn the minimum necessary for subsistence, which has recently been going up at a dizzying rate.

In this respect (as in many others, incidentally) the fate of the Theatre of the Rain and its creators is no exception. Most of the new theatre studios that appeared in the 1980s in one of the world's leading cultural centres, St Petersburg, arose and exist in these straitened circumstances.

"What is it that keeps you going?" I asked Natasha Nikitina at the end of our talk. "Enthusiasm? Fanatical devotion?"

"No!" she replied, with a laugh. "It's just that the theatre is a kind of ecological niche for us, a kind of home, that none of us could build just on our own. And people can't do without a home. So we've united to live together in the theatre. And we regard our audiences as members of the family (in spirit, of course, not blood relatives).

After all, the family is the nucleus of the state, as we were always taught at school. So we are a very real and serious force."

Theatre of dreams

The Osobnyak ("Apart") Theatre is, first and foremost, a purely Russian phenomenon in the way it grew up and operates. For several years a small team of four people (Igor Larin, T. Krekhno, O. Teterina and D. Podzorov), all professionally trained actors, existed "nowhere", if one might put it like that, playing once or twice a season at various festivals. These rare sorties into the public were invariably accompanied by sensational (sometimes even scandalous) success, and it began to look as if now that public interest was aroused everything would sort itself out. But nothing did, and the theatre continued to lead a kind of mythical way of life, to exist while not existing. The public could not (even if they wanted to) go and see their productions for the simple reason that there was nowhere to go. The unemployed actors obviously had no "spare capital" for leasing premises where their productions could be put on regularly. But when it got so bad that they couldn't even afford a proper meal, one of them decided to find a job as caretaker. When he went to apply for it, he had a very frank conversation with the manager of the local accommodation office. The young man confessed that he was really an actor and that what he wanted most of all was to put on plays with his friends. The manager was so sympathetic that he gave them permission there and then (without filling in any forms or paying any money) to use the so-called "red corner" that belonged to the office.

And so it happened that in the spring of 1992 on Petrograd Side (i.e., one of the city's most prestigious districts) a new theatre studio opened its doors. There were no celebrations or even elementary announcements of this event. Simply on the corner of Ul. Professora Popova and Kirovsky (now Kamennoostrovsky) Prospekt, where the governmental route runs, a rather unimpressive home-made board appeared one morning with the word "OSOBNYAK" in poker-work on it. The sight of it makes you feel that traditional Russian anguish so like an orphan's inconsolable grief. And when you catch sight of the sheet of rain-drenched paper flapping in the wind on which someone has hastily scribbled the date and name of the Osobnyak's next production, you feel so sorry for them that it brings tears to your eyes.

These are hardly the noble elements which one usually associates with the concept of the Theatre. You feel like begging for alms… But the Osobnyak productions are free of charge, because the theatre does not actually have the legal right to exist. Nevertheless, this somewhat dubious status does not stop the official press from writing about the theatre on the same footing as all the others. Although there can hardly be any question of equality, when everything about the Osobnyak is back to front, that is to say, not like it is anywhere else, which to some extent epitomises the Russian way of life.

The prime cause of the many inadequacies (which do not simply accompany, but actually constitute the Osobnyak Theatre) are its productions.

On the one hand, these productions bear no relation to established theatre aesthetics which have become not only traditional, but also stagnant. On the other, being more reminiscent of laboratory experiments than finished masterpieces of theatrical art, they nevertheless contain within them an intonation which is perfectly in keeping with the present day. This is found par excellence in Igor Larin who, as a rule, both directs and designs production (having graduated at the Institute of Architecture before moving on to the Theatre Institute) and also plays the lead in them. Larin even thought up the theatre's name.

The name Osobnyak comes more from the adverbial slang meaning of the word ("standing apart") than the noun ("a detached house") And the favourite genre of the theatre's production is the DREAM, a dream full of unexpected visions and illusions, nightmares and absurd concatenations. The dream as an attempt to embody the collective unconsciousness, to give it form albeit briefly in the extremely ephemeral matter of the actor's play, which can hardly be called matter in the accepted sense of the word.

Naturally, both the logic of the plot and the characters which arise on the stage during the productions are, like dreams, as whimsical and unreal as our nocturnal visions. Yet this unlifelike form is precisely what makes it possible to dismember those essential relations which organise life itself.

The first opus of this kind arose as a result of their production of Chekhov's play *The Cherry Orchard*, which has recently become quite fashionable thanks to perestroika and appears regularly on the stages of many theatres in Moscow and Petersburg each season.

Igor Larin's production is called *The Cherry Orchard Dream*. It begins with theatregoers being greeted as they come in by a lady in a black silk dress, whose face is hidden by a heavy veil. "Come along, come along," she invites you in a hollow voice. Everything is according to etiquette, yet shivers run down your spine.

The people find their seats and the lights go down. The lady in black turns out to be a "museum guide". In her hollow voice she proposes to introduce them to the life of the gentry in the last century. On the stage is a huge cube with an aluminium frame containing the remains of a house, judging by the situation, the one in which Ranevskaya used to live. A young man in a greatcoat is sitting some distance away from this geometrical structure and blowing a trumpet rather excruciatingly.

After a few minutes out of the ruins rise the "museum exhibits", the gentlefolk themselves or rather their ghosts. Ranevskaya is wearing a long white shift, vaguely reminiscent of a strait-jacket, and has a haggard face, dark hollow cheeks and short tangled hair as if she has just woken up.

Meanwhile the appearance of Ranevskaya transforms the two who are already on the stage. The "lady in black" shakes a bundle of keys in her hand which is enough for the audience to recognise Varya, Ranevskaya's adopted daughter, a lonely old maid who has been hopelessly in love with Lopakhin for many years. But her heart is now so constricted by life (like her body by the black dress) that she seems incapable of feeling anything at all.

From Varya's lips we hear only scraps of Chekhov's lines. She could not keep quiet, of course, when Ranevskaya appeared. Lopakhin (who is the young man playing the trumpet all the time) makes a beeline for Lyubov Andreyevna, the landowner, almost knocking Varya the housekeeper over on the way, but not noticing her. Now he has even less time for his "fiancee", because he discovers that the cube is made of glass, so he (Lopakhin) not only cannot go up to Ranevskaya and touch her, but cannot even be heard by her (everyone knows that he is crazy about her, quite besotted), but they exist in different worlds, cut off from each other. And, like the hero, the audience see this with their own eyes, because it is demonstrated clearly on the stage. Spread-eagled on the "glass" (there is actually no glass at all, it is only "acted") of the cube which is protecting the "museum exhibit", Lopakhin sinks down in a long and painful movement and collapses on the floor, furious at his own helplessness.

At this point Ranevskaya's brother, Gayev, appears in the cube, or rather a kind of ghost of the man, an amusing "plaster cast" of a theatricalised marquis. He and Ranevskaya try to remember their lines, chanting scraps from well-known dialogues like sleep-walkers. Gayev mutters his famous monologue almost to himself, addressing the ruins, with his back to the audience. Then he and Ranevskaya take each other by the hand, like little children, and begin gravely and carefully to dance a minuet, as they were taught in childhood. During this dance-reminiscence a man with red cheeks who looks like an itinerant actor pops up out of the ruins and with the assistance of some crudely made puppets proceeds deftly and briskly to act the dialogues in Chekhov's play between Anya and Petya and Yasha and Dunyasha, and show Charlotta performing her tricks, etc. Ranevskaya suddenly breaks off her mechanical dance to watch the play and her sad smile gradually turns into a malevolent grimace. Gayev also watches the play and with his characteristic childlike impulsiveness is so impressed and carried away by the action that he tries to take part in it. When the "valet Yasha" puppet raises his "despicable voice" Gayev, shouting the completely meaningless phrase "there's a smell of chicken", tries to hit Yasha, whom he dislikes strongly, with his stick.

Throughout this action which takes place inside the cube (and makes it look increasingly like an aquarium with decorative fish darting around inside) Lopakhin gets more and more tense and rushes round the glass walls trying in vain to catch Ranevskaya's attention. At one moment he even seems to succeed: Lyubov Andreyevna notices him, opens her eyes wide and walks up to the transparent, but insuperable barrier. Heartened by her attention, Lopakhin makes feverish attempts to save this woman whom he adores, by repeating time and time again that all they need do is cut down the cherry orchard. Ranevskaya smiles back at him, obviously not understanding what he has said. His words simply cannot be heard through the glass.

This almost lovers' dialogue is cut short by a new emotional outburst from Varya, who all this time has been sitting on a chair at the side, like a museum attendant, knitting an endless black scarf. Only now she starts acting like a frontier guard: catching her "victim" in the narrow beam of a searchlight, she orders him in a harsh metallic voice to stand back from the exhibit. This sends Lopakhin into hysterics. Going down heavily on one knee in front of her, he screams furiously: "Ochmelia! Get thee to a nunnery!" His anger with his "black bride" grows all the more intense and pointless as he realises the impossibility of what he really wants – to be with the people inside the glass cube, who have a completely different life which is not accessible to him and therefore very attractive.

This constant discrepancy between what he wants and what he has finally comes to a head, like an abcess, triggered off by a formal reason: everything, as always, is suddenly a matter of money.

In the following scene when Ranevskaya, complaining for the nth time about not having enough money, accidentally drops her purse (one which we and the actress imagine), the sound of heavy coins (also imaginary, of course) dropping from the skies gradually fills the whole stage. And at this point Lopakhin forgets about Lyubov Andreyevna and for the first time in the whole action stops gazing at her, even loses sight of her completely. His face transformed, he pulls off his greatcoat and throws it onto the ground leaving himself free to pick up the heavy "drops" of gold rain. Crawling around on his knees, he tries to rake together the money with his arms, but his efforts are in vain, because in fact there is no money. It is all a mirage. The coins go on falling, accompanied by the characteristic sound, only to vanish as unexpectedly as they appeared.

Scene from *The Cherry Orchard Dream* at the Osobnyak Theatre. Photo: Sergei Smirnov.

The inhabitants of the aquarium stand in a row at the front watching in amazement the strange behaviour of the man clutching at thin air. Lopakhin sobs loudly, and the more convulsed his movements, the fainter and less frequent the sound of falling coins.

In the total silence which eventually follows Lopakhin smashes the cube with a frenzied blow of his fist. There is a sound of breaking glass, and, carried along by the momentum of his blow, he falls slowly (as if in a dream or oblivion) into the cube, driving out its permanent inhabitants, who just as slowly (as if in a dream or oblivion) find themselves in a medium which is strange and alien to them. Their confusion is heightened by an excruciating gnashing sound that is cut short by silence, which in turn gives way to a blinding electric light…

And at this moment when the tension is at its height a woman in the audience starts complaining loudly that it's wrong to distort the great Chekhov like this, that the whole production is a disgrace, and so on and so forth. She rushes out of the hall, slamming the door behind her. But no one in the audience supports this custodian of the purity of Russian literature, although they watch her behaviour fascinated. (Many of them probably realise that she was planted in the audience.)

Meanwhile, when the audience's attention returns to the stage where some significant changes have taken place. The commoner Lopakhin cannot forgive the gentry for the humiliation he has experienced in front of them and, as he believes, through their fault. So he decides to get his own back! He is the boss now. He is in charge, dressed in a bright blue service jacket trimmed with gold, and his hair slicked back. But the most important thing, of course, is the way his personality has changed. His voice is authoritative, his movements few and precise. In general he is the complete opposite of the poor young man in the greatcoat who was struggling to get into the aquarium-cube not so long ago.

When the former owners of the cherry orchard are taking their leave of Lopakhin he invites them to have some champagne, taking four test tubes of a lurid red liquid out of his pocket. "Do have some, ladies and gentlemen!" In the strong white light (resembling a single naked light bulb in an empty room) Ranevskaya looks incredibly like the inmate in a prison camp, although she is holding her test-tube very elegantly. Lopakhin makes one final attempt to declare his devotion to Lyubov Andreyevna, but, confronted by her no longer surprised, but all-knowing, bitter expression, he bursts out laughing like a madman and pours the contents of his test-tube demonstratively onto the floor.

All the "has-beens", i.e., Ranevskaya, Gayev and the "puppeteer", who represents the other inhabitants of the estate, gradually recede into the background. Their submissive steps and resigned bearing suggest the idea of their death. And they do in fact vanish into the darkness, as the lights on the stage gradually go down.

The lady in black quickly puts dust-covers over the broken exhibit with "relics of the past". And the excursion is over.

Lopakhin, now in a kind of withdrawn trance, pulls on his old greatcoat, picks up his trumpet and, as if he has suddenly noticed the audience for the first time, says to them: "Out you go, ladies and gentlemen.

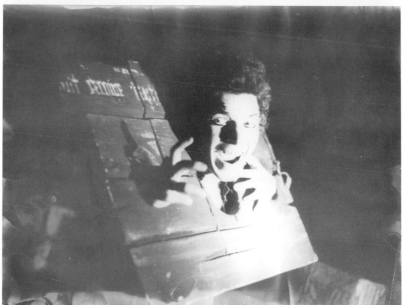

Scenes from the mime-ballet *The Temptation of St Jerome*. Photo: Sergei Smirnov.

Goodbye!" And goes on until the audience, somewhat taken aback and confused by the fact that they have not even been allowed to applaud and thus draw the line between the stage and life, separate themselves from what has taken place on the stage, troop off obediently towards the exit.

This joyless theatre farewell is accompanied by the melancholy sounds of a solitary trumpet.

Igor Larin's impressive production stays in your mind for a long time. What is more, it has a remarkably strong after-taste to which you keep returning: and the unusual treatment of Chekhov's play is no less riveting than the original scenic form in which it is embodied.

The creators of *The Cherry Orchard Dream* have defined its form with the somewhat inexpressive term "mime-ballet". This term is a most doubtful one, of course, but one is bound to agree that it does express, to some extent at least, the essence of the matter. What we see before us is, indeed, a kind of "mime-ballet", although none of the characters here even thinks of dancing, apart from the strange recollection of their childhood by Ranevskaya and Gayev, which develops into something resembling a minuet. What we see before us is, indeed, a kind of "mime-ballet", even though there is hardly any music at all in the production and it certainly does not predetermine either the movements or the behaviour of the characters. What we see before us is an unusual form of "mime-ballet" for the simple reason that absolutely all the relations which arise between the characters are realised in powerful plastic images which are constantly present and developing on the stage. Igor Larin "uses" Chekhov's play to stage the production more as a libretto, on the basis of which the director creates the fabric of the scenic text, than as a hallowed literary foundation, which the actors simply intone from the stage, presumably on the assumption that this is enough for a play by the great playwright.

Just over a year later the Osobnyak repertoire acquired another production which continued the quest in the sphere of "mime-ballet". In fact, it was even called *An Evening of Mime-Ballet*. The *Evening* consists of two sections, the first (*The Temptation of St Jerome*) being based on the paintings by Bosch and Breughel and the second (*Petrushka*) on "Russian motifs". And although the stylistics of the pictorial elements are extremely different (Bosch, Breughel and chapbooks would not appear to go well together) both sections combined with each other most organically.

As in *The Cherry Orchard Dream*, the characters in the "mime-ballets" are not people, but "fragments" of people. Here they barely communicate on the level of words, uttering only disconnected sounds. Each of them has been "battered" by life, so to say, and each has remained in that state for the rest of his or her life. Some are aggressive, others very sad, but there are rebels too. They are all united by a definite onesidedness, a fixation on one particular emotion (or even one particular

Igor Larin's mono-play *Confessions of a Baron*. Photo: Sergei Semyonov.

Igor Larin's mono-play *My First Friend*. Photo: Sergei Semyonov.

movement), one particular urge, which, judging by everything, has remained unfulfilled in their real life. This fixation generates "strange", although very understandable and easily recognised forms of behaviour and interaction between the characters. For example, in "Jerome" there is a character whose chest has been pierced all the way through by an arrow. He exists in this state all the time. But he did not acquire it (the state) on the battlefield in a particular battle. The wound he bears was inflicted not by an enemy or rival, but by life itself.

Or in *Petrushka* – a greedy merchant gets hold of a doll-like beauty and even marries her into the bargain, but as a result we see the following scene: the merchant puts the beautiful girl on his back which makes her legs stick up into the air (a doll does not have flexible joints; thus she is given her "position" in life space), and begins, bent triple, to carry his "doll" along the road of life, as his cross, his wife-burden, whereas the "doll" does not bat an eyelid and keeps the same vacant coquettish expression on her face as before, the only difference being that she is now upside down.

The *Evening of Mime-Ballet* is acted by four unemployed actors: T. Krekhno, O. Teterina, D. Podzorov and Igor Larin, who as well as acting, still continues to direct and design the Osobnyak productions. On top of this Igor Larin (entirely "for himself") creates literary compositions (on the friendship between Pushkin and Pushchin – *My First Friend*, on the life of Alexander Vertinsky – *Confessions of a Baron*, and *Darkening* based on Dostoyevsky's novel *Crime and Punishment*) and acts monoplays based on them for audiences in the small theatre hall of the St Petersburg Theatre Museum, where he once worked first as a fireman, then as a caretaker. He does not get paid for this, of course, but they are very fond of him there. They print his posters for him, let him use the hall free of charge, give him tea after the performances, and if they can afford it also a present for his small son.

With his passion for directing Igor has recently begun making a serious study of the work of Meyerhold and Mikhail Chekhov. They have become guiding stars in Igor's new profession (he studied in the acting faculty of the St Petersburg Theatre Institute).

It is probably worth mentioning that the additional and very serious efforts made by the director of the Osobnyak Theatre Studio concern the sphere of artistic interests only, and therefore do not affect the company's financial situation. Today all the actors (and not only one "lucky one") now work as caretakers.

These "caretakers" of ours are being invited more and more frequently to international festivals. One cannot help being pleased at their success, of course, but also saddened because the Osobnyak's rare meetings with the St Petersburg public have now become even rarer, thanks to these tours abroad.

At the same time this "invisible theatre" gets a bigger press than anyone else, and when they give an interview its creators always manage to insert something like: "We'll still go on acting our productions whatever the circumstances of our life."

From my talk to Igor Larin I realised that this position is certainly not based on fanaticism. It is simply that before they got together in the Osobnyak each of these actors had worked in the state theatre system and did not want to do so anymore. They are prepared to work as caretakers, but in the theatre they want to create something, not about life over there, but about the corrupt life with which their audience, their contemporaries and fellow-countrymen, are unfortunately only too familiar.

Private life in the show genre

The biography of Terrà Mobile is full of paradoxes. Take the fate of its director, Vadim Mikheyenko, for example. He graduated from the Leningrad Theatre Institute in the early seventies, then worked as a actor for a long time trying to find himself on the professional stage (in the capital and in provincial theatres as well). But as a result of these many years of work he earned not an apartment and a car, but a rare form of allergy. After many trials and tribulations, when the doctors gave him up completely as a hopeless case, Vadim actually managed to cure himself. Today he recommends this prescription to everyone: apparently all you need to do is leave the state theatre system and that does the trick!

Terra Mobile does not call itself a theatre. It is a "creative association" which arose thanks to the personal initiative of Vadim Mikheyenko. He appointed himself as its designer and director.

But here's another paradox. Mikheyenko's ten years in charge of his own collective has resulted in a Terra repertoire which consists of two productions only – a SHOW programme and "Private Life". And the two are very closely linked, one production overflowing into the other. Looking at the situation from the formal point of view, it is quite impossible to understand how with such insignificant results Terra has been able to win the main prizes at all the mime and plastic theatre festivals over the last few years like clockwork. And no one even dreamed of accusing it of being unproductive or resting on its laurels.

To understand what this is all about we must go back to the very beginning. The first step was when a few young people got together and started to do break dancing. In the mid-eighties this dance was at the height of its popularity in our country and it really put Terra on the map. The team acquired the status of a professional variety ensemble which not only performed in Leningrad, but toured the whole vast Soviet Union with tremendous success. At that time it really was a type of ensemble which required not only a similar level of performing skill, but also a unity of performing style. Everyone here looked the same, which attracted audiences by its modern image.

Fashion is never wrong, even if it looks hideous in relation to accepted criteria of beauty; it is always right, because it is the most faithful reflection of the day. And in break dancing the basic conflict of modern man is encoded and deciphered at the same time. The conflict between the need for a strictly regulated and therefore stereotyped existence and the individual's urge to be unique.

On the one hand, break dancing is characterised by robot-like movements which must be performed by all the dancers in unison; yet

Nikolai Kurushin and Larissa Naumova in Terra Mobile's *Private Life*. Photo courtesy of Nikolai Kurushin.

each is closed not only by the sameness of the mechanical movements, but also by dark glasses on their eyes and gloves on their hands. The break dancer is packaged, so to say.

On the other hand, break dancing, like many group dances, is based on the principle of competition, when each dancer tries to demonstrate a more complicated and polished trick than his rival in order to show how unique and original he is! This element, which makes break dancing particularly attractive to young people, of course, involves impulsiveness and bursts of energy which really send the audience, as they themselves admit.

Break dancing creates a very precise image of the present day, but this image is always the same and, moreover, an extremely general one.

It is hard to say now exactly when, how and which of the members of the Terra Mobile creative association was the first to sense not only the value of break dancing, but also the limitations of its imagery which produced a too general view of the key problem of the present day. But at one of the "mime-panoramas" held in Leningrad in the late eighties, the team showed an experimental work that later became the central episode in the production *Private Life*. It was a plastic duet, in

Finale of *Private Life*. Photo: Vadim Mikheenko.

which He and She took part, characters who could hardly be called break dancers even by a long stretch of the imagination. Firstly, the sign depiction of the conflict recorded with the help of plastico-rhythmic hieroglyphs gave way to graphic strokes in an attempt to create a typological portrait. Secondly, the actual conflict itself changed. This time the opposing forces, although weak, were personified: the Man was dressed in a suit, a white shirt and a tie, while the Woman's body was in a tight-fitting "ballet" leotard. Protectedness and Unprotectedness clashed and, as in the eternal collision between the male and female elements, neither would give way or even attempt to understand the other.

In this duet the actors do not simply demonstrate a problem and try to study it. In their movements you can easily detect the break dancing mood, but no more. The stylistics of their behaviour are extremely simple, almost ordinary and naturalistic. Here they are, both young and good-looking, standing side by side to get married. Then the "position"

Terra Mobile's show programme "What am I to do? There are tanks in the town..." (Terra Mobile).

of their relationship to life changes, like a still in a film. Now only He is in front, while her gentle bare arms, which have appeared from behind his back, embrace his neck, stroke his chest and, finally, clamp together in an "iron" lock. From now onwards He is the husband and She is the wife. He starts to walk, dragging her along on his back, and going for-wards at first, but then in a circle, or rather following the path of the "circular" sameness of the relations produced by these marital ties. Each stage of this endless running around in a circle is harder than the one before. And so it goes on until both characters, and both actors too, reach an extra-aesthetic ugliness which perhaps only the totally "naturalistic" movement of a physically exhausted person can produce.

Then comes a new frame, heralding the beginning of a new episode and a new cycle in these people's relationship. But we do not enter it as abruptly as the first time, with the help of an instantaneous clip, but gradually, "tricked" by the plastic and psychological substitution. The Man tries to seat the exhausted Woman on a chair, in an effort to help her, as it were. An ordinary, personal impulse, one would think. But She takes it as an act of coercion (there is even a hint of sexual abuse here) and resists desperately, sliding from the chair onto the floor. A bitter, exhausting struggle ensues, fired by mutual misunderstanding, which goes on for so long that it begins to seem endless, eternal, involving more than just these two people. And as a result we have the familiar picture of extreme devastation, exhaustion, despair and longing which prostrate the two characters.

The appearance of this experimental work marked the beginning of a change in Terra's creative orientation. They did not abandon break dancing which had brought them together, but they were now aware that the most valuable thing in the world is the individual.

They began this new programme of self-realisation with themselves. And nearly broke up, because it resulted almost at once in the appearance of a repertoire in various different styles, consisting for the most part of short numbers. Yasha Malkin improvised some amusing mimed sketches, Igor Naumov went over to parodies of breakers, Tatiana Volkova continued serious breaking, and Stanislav Varkke and Nikolai Kurushin tried to learn rap, but instead of using well-known English texts, they made up their own in Russian (which is how the very popular "What can I do? There are tanks in the town..." and "Lots of folk are drinking compote" appeared). Varkke, this time together with Larissa Naumova, mastered art nouveau ballet and rehearsed the number "Homecoming" about the Soviet troops who fought in Afghanistan. In short, everyone started to do their own thing.

And what about Vadim Mikheyenko, Terra's producer and artistic director?

As far as I can see, in this story of the logical appearance of creative demarcation (which takes place in any team sooner or later), Mikheyenko adopted the wisest of all possible courses: he welcomed everything and everyone.

Sensing intuitively that perhaps the most characteristic feature of our life today is the eclectic style of existence, when grandma's iron trunk co-exists happily with a Japanese video camera, and a piece of dry bread with some delicious morsel from a humanitarian aid consignment sent by friends abroad, etc., Mikheyenko decided that the audience of today would understand and appreciate productions based on the same principle of eclectic combination of everything life produces. So he began to compose collage-plays.

As soon as the results of creative experiment by any Terra people reached a certain state, they were immediately included for general approbation in a SHOW programme which, by its very nature, assumed the combination of very different types of material on different levels. If the number passed the test of the SHOW programme, with time (and not without changes, of course) it appeared in the production "Private Life". So this explains why it is that the Terra Mobile repertoire consists of only two productions after all this time, but that both of them are permanently having first nights.

Terra audiences caught on to this at once. Probably because they too have a very paradoxical feature: people go to see Terra productions over and over again, not just once. So the audience is immersed together with the actors in a kind of unusual shared journey through life, as it were. This constant contact (unlike the usual practice of seeing a play once only) gives the audience a sense of taking part in everything Terra does.

In spite of the fact that Terra has never had posters because of its financial state, and that they play wherever they can through lack of their own "house", the productions put on by this "creative association" are always an unqualified success.

In the last few years, since Russia's frontiers have opened up slightly for her citizens, Terra has started going abroad each summer for three or four months. But paradoxically these trips can hardly be called foreign tours.

No one in the west (apart from the Jerzy Grotowski school) has ever opened the door to Terra and invited them to cross the threshold. The actors perform in the streets and squares there, sometimes dancing break, sometimes simply standing like live mechanical dolls, and more rarely improvising on themes of plastic compositions from their productions. Their summer earnings enable them to come back to Russia and spend several months rehearsing like mad so as to bag the prizes at all the festivals.

In 1991 unexpectedly for many a new production was added to the Terra repertoire. Paradoxical though it may seem, they breaked their way to putting on Gogol's *overcoat*.

This production makes no attempt to tell the story of the poor civil servant Akaky Akakievich Bashmachkin. What we see is one man

trying to survive, who finds himself in opposition to the rest. Not inten-
tionally (he is not a hero at all), but simply because he does not know the
universally accepted rules of the game. So he keeps slipping out of the
complex rhythmical and plastic patterns typical of break dance compositions. Until his life comes to a tragic end, like that of the main character
in Gogol's story.

The *overcoat* continues the structural principle begun in *Private
Life*. It too is constructed like a show, and the numbers that make it up
change from time to time. Nothing fixed or rigid, in other words, "Terra
mobile".

In search of the fire to make the omelette

The Formal Theatre literally descended onto the heads of the Petersburg public. No one knew or wished to know of its existence until the first festival of new theatre studios took place in June 1990. The festival was organised by what was then still the Leningrad section of the Union of Theatre Workers with the aim of discovering (and, if possible, also supporting) such theatres. The Formal Theatre filled in its application to take part the day before the festival was due to open, after reading a short newspaper announcement about it.

Festival audiences are always special. To say that they are keen theatregoers is not enough. They are people for whom the theatre is the be-all and end-all, people who live for the theatre. So just imagine what one of these well-wishers (or members of the jury, for example) would feel like if they got biffed on the head with a stick as they were entering the foyer on their way to the festival!

The stick was just a prop, of course, not a real one, and could not have caused an injury, but at that particular moment a person might experience not only confusion, but various other far from pleasant emotions as well.

And it was precisely this challenging and somewhat clumsy joke, which could not possibly be ignored, that the Formal Theatre used to announce its arrival, not eliciting an over enthusiastic response from the public thereby. True, ten days later, when the festival reached its end, it was this team with Andrei Moguchy's production of "The Bald Prima Donna" that was universally acclaimed the winner.

Ionesco's play centres, as we know, around two married couples who are identical to the point of absurdity. In Moguchy's production the high degree of absurdity which is inherent in the play was expanded by the producer to universal proportions. In the course of the action (or rather lack of it, because in fact nothing happens between these people nor can it happen as they are actually no longer people at all) the actors and actresses changed parts, even playing members of the opposite sex, without in any way affecting the meaning.

Yet the special significance and attraction of Moguchy's production lay in more than this. One might even say that Moguchy used Ionesco's text merely as an excuse to make a frank statement of his own, because the main meaning of the production emerged when the text of the French dramatist's play ended. The "second" part of the production opened with the appearance of a real live rooster on the stage. The elemental naturalness of this living creature immediately provided a striking contrast to the so-called "people", who are normally regarded as beings of a higher order. The effect of civilisation on these people, which has deprived them of everything humane, looked particularly monstrous beside this innocent domestic bird. The audience received a shock. And at this point Moguchy's production got a kind of second wind. The pace rhythm and stylistics of the action changed radically and it developed into an absolutely wordless metaphor. What actually took place was very simple: sophisticated invention gave way to ordinary reality. Tired from acting the play the actors relaxed and began to take off the "alien" clothes and wigs and remove the makeup profusely laced with sweat from their faces. The lush theatrical rhetoric receded, as if it had never existed, and into the silence that replaced it came real life. The glare of the footlights also began to recede slowly, and someone lit a candle. Its solitary flame looked defenceless yet also full of the life force, like the semi-naked bodies of the people gathered round the flickering light. For a while this resembled a "mythological scene": man and fire, or even mankind and fire. In their imagination the audience were carried back into remote antiquity and reminded of Prometheus and the days when man communed with nature tête-à-tête without the intermediacy of developed forms of civilisation. Similar associations came and went until the audience's ears were suddenly "barraged" by rock music. The blare of "heavy metal" forced us back to the modern world. The sound, although musical, lashed our minds with such force that it seemed intolerable. Liberation came unexpectedly: a window, masked in a wall, flew open, and the blinding light of day flooded into the room together with a gust of fresh air, breaking into the hitherto closed and confined space.

And in the window appeared a figure wearing long white, loose-fitting robes. Everyone was mesmerised by it—actors and audience alike. But unlike the audience, the actors were drawn towards it physically and disappeared one by one, as if in a trance following the mysterious visitor in the stream of fresh air blowing through the window. For the audience their "disappearance" was yet another shock, because they knew perfectly well that the room in which the performance was taking place, was on the first floor.

For a while the mesmerised audience stayed in their seats, but eventually natural curiosity got the better of them and they all rushed to the window. In time to see a group of people walking off into the distance over the rubbish-strewn wasteland of a building site, their eyes fixed on the horizon and the slowly setting sun.

This symbolic exodus from the theatre which summed up their first premiere was to be most prophetic for the subsequent fate of the "Formal Theatre". At first their posters announced more and more new productions, which should have led to the building up of a theatre repertoire. Ionesco's *Bald Prima Donna* was followed by productions of Tom

Stoppard's *Rosencrantz and Guildenstern are Dead*, Sam Shepard's *Fool for Love*, a dramatisation of Andrei Bely's novel *Petersburg* and *Two Sisters* (based on Turgenev).

At the same time Andrei Moguchy kept insisting that "Our theatre is not a theatre at all!" And in fact he was striving not to put on regular and frequent performances of ready-made plays, but to organise rare theatricalised actions with a powerful impact.

One could have predicted such a turn way back in the days of the first festival of theatre studios, when on a St Petersburg white night, on the famous Strelka on Vassilievsky Island, the "Formalists" erected from ordinary scaffolding a kind of multi-storey pyramidal construction consisting of five square blocks to act out Dostoyevsky's *Crime and Punishment*. Act being the operative word, because each of the blocks forming a stage was given a name: "Rodya the student", "I've brought something to pawn, Alyona Ivanonva, here it is…", "'I didn't kill her…' 'Yes, you did, Rodion Romanovich, it was you, sir…'" "'Go and confess, Rodya.' 'Alright, Sonya, I'm going'" and finally "So we're both going the same way … come on then".

Not only the principle of organising the acting space, which is divided up into "frames", but also the style of the acting itself in this performance (it is impossible to call it a play) reminds one of a film. The actors exist in the stylistics of the silent film, depicting a fairly unambivalent "mime". First one "frame" comes to life, then it "freezes" and the action moves to the next one. And so on to the end, then it starts all over again, from beginning to end, and could theoretically go on for ever. The pattern of the "picture" inside each block never changes, but the audience's reaction becomes more and more emotionally charged with each repetition.

It was after this performance of Dostoyevsky that the now fashionable term "post-modernism" began to be used in discussions about the Formal Theatre.

Yet Andrei Moguchy is firmly opposed to any attempt to restrict the activity of his team, particularly when people try to contain it within the narrow framework of this or that fashionable term. At this point it would probably be best to let Andrei speak for himself:

"I first became interested in the theatre when I was a student at the Leningrad Institute of the Aviation Industry. It was one of the technical colleges which in the 1970s produced not so many well-trained engineers as composers, writers, actors and directors, people active in the arts. I went there to please my parents. It was the custom in our family to give children a good education and a respectable profession (my mother is a lawyer and my father a doctor). I did my bit at the institute and even got a diploma in engineering, but all the time I was learning about the theatre. So when I graduated and managed in spite of the regulations not to work for a certain number of years as an engineer (my work record has got all sorts of strange entries in it), I did an external course at the faculty of direction in the Leningrad Krupskaya Institute of Culture. People say external courses are no good, but I thought it was excellent that for half the year we students each did what we liked in our studios and then went over it during the exams with experienced teachers.

The studio which I organised after I began work as director of student amateur dramatics at the Aviation Industry Institute was called the experimental theatre studio. This was at the very beginning of the eighties, when a great deal was still forbidden in our country. And like many of our contemporaries we found what was illegal (up to and including means of subsistence) far more attractive than what was allowed, official. For example, we were dead against Stanislavsky and wouldn't even hear his name mentioned. Today his books have become like the Bible to me, but then we were all interested in the writings of Jerzy Grotowski and Michael Chekhov, and in general everything that was ignored or rejected by our official and semi-official theatres.

We stayed underground for several years. We had no great urge to come out and perform to the public at large, preferring our own audiences, albeit not very large, but consisting of our friends and acquaintances, who could be trusted and who trusted us.

Our most important task was to create a theatre by finding, not destroying, ourselves with the help of the acting profession. We discovered quite a lot in those days which we are still using today. When we began giving regular performances to the public we had to make some changes, of course, but we will never agree to subject ourselves to the laws of the commercial theatre. I understood this properly for the first time when, in search of a salary (due to being permanently skint), my friends and I went to work with an American troupe. This episode was so alien and so unsettling for us, that for a long time the material gain could not compensate for the moral damage which we suffered.

The Americans chose us because we were rumoured to be post-modernists who liked putting on "performances". But dragging out as many literary quotations as possible is not the main thing, as I see it. (We're all so well-read these days, that we can quote anything you like, even post-modernist texts). As somebody once said (I don't remember who, but I really like it): post-modernism is a bit like an omelette Bulgarian style, where you throw in eggs, ham, onion, tomatoes, peppers and whatever else you may have, in other words, totally eclectic. But unless you can find the fire to cook the omelette it will just look pretty and be quite inedible. Likewise a "performance" (even if it is most imaginatively constructed) will never become a work of art if there is no fire in the hearts of the people who created it.

The Formal Theatre's production of *People, Lions, Eagles and Partridges* ... based on the non-existent play by Konstantin Treplev. Photo: Alexei Danichev.

The Formal Theatre's production of *People, Lions, Eagles and Partridges...* based on the non-existent play by Konstantin Treplev. Photo: Alexei Danichev.

I don't like it when people try to limit the theatre to the narrow framework of this or that term. A theatre is like a person. As long as it is alive, it has the right (even the duty) to change from day to day. For example, we called ourselves the Formal Theatre and now we regret it. It's too late to change, because people are used to it, but it does orientate the public a priori in a definite way and that is a nuisance."

The prospectuses and posters that accompany productions by the Formal Theatre refer to one and the same title sometimes as a performance and sometimes as a play. I think the second term is more fitting, because a "performer", as we know, does not have to be an actor, that is, to play a part, and in the Formal Theatre that situation does not arise. The fact is that our way of acting and also our way of organising the artistic text is quite unorthodox.

It is interesting that in awarding this team first prize, the jury suggested that it be called the Konstantin Treplev prize, after the character in Chekhov's *Seagull* who keeps saying all the time: "We need new forms. New forms are what we need. And if there aren't any, we don't need anything."

Konstantin Treplev's idea appealed to the "Formalists" so much that with time Andrei Moguchy and his team put on Treplev's play *People,*

Lions, Eagles and Partridges… A play which does not exist! It has never been written by anybody, but is merely referred to in Chekhov's comedy.

The structure of this super-untraditional play consisted of mixing two collages at once. One of them was a compilation of quotations from several Chekhov plays (*The Seagull, Three Sisters*, and *The Cherry Orchard*); the other of stage directions from earlier Formal Theatre productions (*The Bald Prima Donna, Petersburg* and *Rosencrantz and Guildenstern are Dead*).

The scenic action was made up of simultaneously coexisting episodes. None of them had a developed plot, but resembled a slowly developing and sometimes constantly changing motif, containing a deliberately obvious traditional idea of literary characters and the situations connected with them.

A man in a peasant shirt and boots is cutting down trees with an axe. And everyone realises straightaway that it is Lopakhin from *The Cherry Orchard*, the only character in the play who knows how to live.

Here are three young women chatting animatedly among themselves and singing, as they perform an endless, tedious job. They are winding some thin coloured thread round a huge metal carcass, trying to create something like the wall of a house. There is no end to this work in sight, but its futility is very obvious. The women's merry laughter gradually turns into hysterics. And everyone realises straightaway that it is Irina, Olga and Masha from *The Three Sisters*, whose dream of a new life has not come true.

And here is a young man wandering about like a lost soul and tossing out high-flown phrases into space, examples of the new art: *People, Lions, Eagles and Partridges…* And everyone realises straightaway that it is the self-same Konstantin Treplev from *The Seagull*.

A romantically inclined young lady is "flying" to and fro on a swing. She is like a mysterious bird, her dress fluttering and her eyes gazing up to the sky full of noble impulses. She is dreaming of a career on the stage and great roles and also of a great love, of course. And everyone realises straightaway that it is Nina Zarechnaya from *The Seagull*.

A group of people are sitting round a big table covered with a white cloth. They are talking endlessly. True, it is impossible to make out what they are saying, but what we see before us is a picture of trusting, intimate communion, which somehow ends unexpectedly with the death of one of those present: a bottle of red wine falls over, staining the tablecloth and the white shirt of one of the characters a deep red.

And everyone realises straightaway that they are typical Chekhovian (and even more broadly Russian) intellectuals, that is to say, people who are essentially noble-hearted, but failures dying of boredom: Arkadina and Trigorin (from *The Seagull*), Ranevskaya (from *The Cherry Orchard*), Tusenbach (from *The Three Sisters*) and so on.

From time to time all these simultaneously coexisting episodes are lit up and drowned by fireworks of exploding crackers. However, the atmosphere of hopelessness is intensified by the mournful moans of a saxophone framed by a rhythmically pulsating electric guitar.

From the very beginning there is a cupboard at the back of the stage (the "precious, most respected cupboard" that is a symbol of a care-free, happy childhood for Ranevskaya and Gayev from *The Cherry Orchard*). This cupboard stands in front of the audience throughout the action and reminds one increasingly of another well-known Chekhov quotation which has now become almost proverbial: "If there's a gun on the wall, it is bound to be fired at some point".

The cupboard "fires" at the end. Each of the characters puts on a plastic cover which looks like the uniform of some creature from outer space and disappears into the depths of the cupboard, which turns out to be a door leading to another world.

None of the Formal Theatre's productions contains a single episode (even an episode!) with a place for Joy, particularly unclouded Joy. The atmosphere of all of them without exception generates a special type of aggression—a melancholy aggression, aware of its own hopeless-ness, yet containing a powerful charge of explosive energy.

A certain amount of aggression is one of the principles of Andrei Moguchy's directing, whose productions invariably presuppose the active mastering, even "capturing" of real living space. They are always performed not in a place specially intended for that purpose, i.e., a the-atre, but in almost any other premises, usually one of Petersburg's beau-tiful mansions, the space of which forms part of the content of Moguchy's productions.

These productions can hardly be said to have a strict structure. They remind one rather of a model of an open system which can be modi-fied without the risk of it being destroyed. For example, if the building has two storeys, the action "spreads" over two floors, if three, then over three. But the same production can overcome the spatial limitations of a single room. This tendency to unusual mimicritic transformations was particu-larly obvious in the production based on improvisations on themes from Andrei Bely's novel *Petersburg*, a production which was a most important event in the city's theatrical life. At the beginning of the 1991/1992 season, that is, shortly after Leningrad was officially renamed St Petersburg again, several theatres (both dramatic and musical) immediately announced their intention of producing a stage version of one of the great novels in Russian literature, which throughout the Soviet period had only appeared very rarely in the artistic life of the city on the Neva and the country as a whole.

From this long and complex novel Andrei Moguchy created a one-act composition, arranging it like a musical work in which polyphony develops according to the principle of cacophony: episodes from Bely's

The Commodore based on *Don Juan* at the Formal Theatre. Photo: Alexei Danichev.

Petersburg are acted in different parts of the stage, not in the order in which they appear in the book, and all at the same time.

As a result of this artificially organised composition of the stage text, the audience was clearly unable to follow the development of the events in the literary text of the novel. At the same time, however, their attention was thus freed for another, no less important task: by the end of the production the individual "scenes" merged together in the mind of the onlooker to form a single image of St Petersburg, a city with a special fate, a city with a unique overworld woven from a mass of enigmas as hard to understand as the "Russian soul" itself.

The Formal Theatre is the only one in St Petersburg to have put on a dramatisation of Bely's novel. And probably always will be, because tackling such a task with the use of traditionally organised dramatic material, traditional direction and traditional acting methods (which is what the state theatres in former Leningrad possess today) is impossible.

Just as it is quite impossible to imagine the Formal Theatre, like the state ones, presenting performances every evening on the same stage.

After first putting on Konstantin Treplev's non-existent (I must repeat!) play *People, Lions, Eagles and Partridges...*, the "Formalists" showed it again shortly afterwards in the St Petersburg Sheremetiev Gardens.

Not long afterwards they were to be seen in the southern town of Sochi, where at the opening of the Kinotavr-93 film festival they presented their own version of *Don Juan*, which was based on a number of plays dealing with this eternal subject. A few months later they did a repeat of *Don Juan* in Gorky Park in Moscow.

Following their return to St Petersburg the theatre presented *The Frenzied Roland*, based on Ariosto, first at the opening of the Video Fair-93, then at the opening of Graphicon-93, the First International Forum of Computer Art, which had as its slogan "In search of a third reality".

So the Formal Theatre, which is constantly changing its location, cannot be called an "itinerant troupe" even in the remotest sense.

Andrei Moguchy's team feel quite at home using the incredibly varied life space of the perestroika era as their stage, any of its nooks and crannies. To do this they need only make it their temporary home, i.e., begin to act in it.

Watching some of the Formal Theatre productions in different urban interiors or exteriors you cannot help recalling Shakespeare's famous lines: "All the world's a stage, and all the men and women merely players." But if you happen to be next to Andrei Moguchy at that moment he will almost certainly "correct" Shakespeare's saying, putting it something like this: "All the world's a stage, and all the men and women merely players, acting players who dream of finding themselves one day at least!" Creating new texts based on ones that are well known is the lifelong passion of this director who runs St Petersburg's Formal Theatre.

Entry by love only

In January 1986 I had this talk with the director of the Litsedei ("Play-Makers") clown-mime theatre, Vyacheslav Polunin:[1]

"In the last two or three years Play-Makers, the theatre you run, has become incredibly popular. Not only with mime lovers, as it always has been, but with the public as a whole. The press has painstakingly recorded the progress of your success in a vast number of publications. There's a note of surprised condescension in these admiring remarks. I don't think that's quite fair, considering the long and hard work you have done with a whole team of people. So in our talk today I would like to hear how you yourself explain and evaluate your success. How did Play-Makers begin? What does it care about? How does it live?

I couldn't help being surprised, for example, during a festival that took place last summer in Moscow, that the "play-makers" (which is what people call your actors as well these days) were in a state of military preparedness constantly, tirelessly, all round the clock. I don't just mean the five or six concerts you gave every day in your so-called free time. None of the actors abandoned their roles even in their few moments of leisure. They were constantly egging each other on to act, trying to involve even accidental bystanders in the play."

"That's pretty much the way we live all the time... We don't have a strict rehearsing routine. We're always at the theatre. And a rehearsal could start at any moment, if someone suddenly gets an interesting idea. Then we all join in and have a go, trying to think up new twists. The rehearsal ends when we've exhausted the idea. And we start painting and planing and sawing and sewing again. By the way, we realised long ago that the costumes we design and make ourselves are much better than those we order from people who don't have much of a clue what makes us tick. In a nutshell, we firmly believe in the principle that everything in the theatre must be inspired by love! And love, as we know, demands constancy.

Our favourite production is never seen by an audience, because we act it just for ourselves about once a month. It is called "Vsyaki-byaki" ("Nasty-basties") for a laugh. Anyone can show anything they think is interesting in any form they like. It could be a ready-made number or just a sketch. The main thing about this is the atmosphere of friendly interest. Any good discovery is immediately taken up by the others and developed. So the creative process really is a collective one.

---

[1]This talk was published in the *Leningradsky Rabochy* weekly on 3 January, 1986.

When you're all friends and want to help one another, competition is awful. Everyone's dying to get on the stage. It happens quite naturally that all the actors know all the numbers and roles, because we are all completely inter-changeable. I regard this as an additional incentive for everyone to be on form. But the main thing about our "Nasties" is that they arouse imagination and creative initiative.

"The advantages of a method of working like that are obvious. But doesn't that do away with the need for a director, which is something Play-Makers productions are occasionally criticised for?"

"Generally speaking I welcome criticism and take careful note of it. But quite honestly I just don't understand it when the critics try to apply exactly the same standards to all artistic phenomena, sometimes totally different ones. To my mind, it would be far more productive to try and understand why if there is a gate a person prefers to climb over the fence, rather than try to force him to use the gate.

There can't be any strict directing in our theatre as a matter of principle. Whole productions and individual miniatures live and change as they go along together with us. What's more, we only put on a production for as long as it continues to develop. We think it's bad if a sketch is acted today exactly as it was yesterday. That means we haven't succeeded in making contact with the audience today. That we have simply reproduced what we were able to do before. Of course, we don't always manage to catch the spirit of the audience. But this is not a question of direction, as I see it, but of the extent to which an actor has mastered his part, the extent to which he has mastered a new situation without harming his temperament. You could say that our little bridges are fragile and temporary. But we get over them so quickly and energetically that they don't have time to collapse. For example, the number "Nizya" ("Stop that!") was hardly rehearsed or directed at all. Lyonya Leikin and I just agreed on the bare bones of the situation: my character wants to do very simple things, like taking a ball or sitting on a chair. But his character watches me all the time and thwarts all my attempts with his wretched "Stop that!" We have always acted this number spontaneously. And its success, I think, lies in the fact that my partner never knows exactly what I will come up with next, although we have to be very finely tuned to each other."

"Being tuned to your partner" is something the "play-makers" are very good at indeed. But this kind of mutual understanding does not arise just like that. It takes time to develop surely?"

"Yes, it does. We began way back at the end of the sixties and, it must be said, rather traditionally. Like many others, we started by imitating Marcel Marceau, who had been touring here just before that. Mime proved to be very infectious and Marceau's authority even more so.

We were prepared to "walk on the spot" and "pull on the rope" day and night. And when we got our act together, we used to perform wherever we were invited, with hardly any thought to what, how and why we were acting. This was the period of blind and all-consuming love."

"I think you are being too hard on your early days. I remember that period very well. For all the naivete in the subjects of your first sketches, they were like a revelation to the audience. It was probably not so much the sketches themselves, but the fact that you managed to convey your love of mime to the audience. And the audience was glad to find out about what was for it a new art at that time. The trouble is that love alone won't get you very far."

"You're so right. There were some big changes just round the corner for us. The new era began when we met Modris Tennison. He started before us and by the mid-sixties he was in charge of one of the first mime troupes in the country, which subsequently went to work at the Kaunas Music and Drama Theatre. We were amateurs, but they were professionals. We had sketches, but they had productions. Our friendship began with terrible arguments about mime. We each had our own ideas about it. But we were very impressed by Tennison's belief that you shouldn't take up the theatre for your own amusement, that a person doesn't have the right to go on the stage until he knows why he is doing it. In other words, he convinced us that the stage should be a pulpit."

"And what effect did this new idea have in practice?"

"Our repertoire remained the same for a while. But things began to change even in our old sketches things. And we ourselves were changing quickly too. We started reading a lot, watched all the old cinema classics again, and got clued up on artistic trends in the theatre... A whole avalanche of impressions! We stopped trying to imitate and selected only what really appealed to us. We were most attracted by folk art and crazy about commedia dell'arte. We were encouraged to start our own quest by Marceau's remark that Chaplin became a genius when he found the right character. Which is true of Marceau himself, when he created his Bip."

I remember that we were constantly (probably even in our sleep) tormented by such questions as "What is a folk hero?", "Why do millions of people love Petrushka, Ivanushka the Fool and Pierrot?" and "Why do people need these characters and what is so attractive about them?"

So we embarked on the task of searching for our own characters. Characters became the central idea of our theatre. Characters that concentrated a whole world inside them and were in tune with the present day.

Each person has his own idea about what is the most important thing in life, so we created all sorts of characters. And the clearer they became, the more we realised that the plot is not the main thing. The main thing is to sustain the logic of the character you have created, but subjects arise naturally out of a clash of characters, the clash of their standpoints.

"And what is your standpoint, the Play-Makers' creed, so to say?"

"A joyful heart! These words contain the essence of our attitude to the world. They define the personality of our collective. I think it is this more than anything else that attracts audiences to us. We inspire them with a thirst for life.

There are at least two more features that our characters have in common. We aim to create them so that they will produce an emotional response. First we tried them out on ourselves. We liked children, so we asked ourselves why it is that any small child, regardless of its character, arouses love, a smile and the desire to communicate with it in those around. Because children are naive and trusting, of course. They are still capable of being surprised and lack stereotypes, boring reactions. And they enjoy finding out about things.

Then another shared feature appeared in our characters, persistence. It appealed to us as well. And, as you can see, it helped us to gradually win respect even from people who didn't understand us. We remembered another saying of Marcel Marceau's: "People's actions outlive them only when the people remain true to their dream."

Our characters did not take shape straightaway, but as they did we grew more and more popular."

"In other words, your work on creating the characters which are present in all your theatre's productions was carried on together with the audience, is that it?"

"Yes, exactly. With the active participation of the audience, who by their reactions—not only by laughing, but also by remaining silent—always conveyed very precisely how moving they found this or that feature in the characters. And depending on the audience reaction we reinforced and developed some things and rejected others."

"I seem to remember that your theatre's dramatic repertoire developed just as gradually, through trial and error, didn't it?"

"It is still basically dependent on the audience or, rather, on the interconnection between the actors and the audience. For the basis of our very existence on the stage is improvisation. The theatre which we preach is a free structure theatre. A "voluntary" theatre, if you like. A character should not have any limitations or it will die, lose its essential spontaneity. Drama should not prevent the actor from improvising. It is on this fine balance between character and drama that we stand. We try to act upon the audience with the help of ideas, but the ideas relate to character, not to the subject. Let me give an example. The subject of the sketch when Asisyai is talking on the phone is not of any intrinsic interest. Two not very young people, each hungry for love, are simply talking. But here not even the words are important (for the most part I make up their dialogue out of gobbledygook). The important thing here is the reaction, the way each of them reacts to the other one's remarks and prepares their own. In order to convey this profound, non-external and non-verbal dialogue, the actor must be fairly free, inter alia, free of drama."

"So each time you go on to the stage you are consciously taking a risk. You are putting yourself in a position where success cannot be guaranteed by previously fixed forms. On the contrary, it is generated literally in accordance with Stanislavsky's formula "the today, here and now", that is, as a result of very close contact between the actors themselves and between the actors and the audience."

"After beginning with a strong interest in classical mime, where much depends on strictness of form and virtuoso technique of movement and in no way doubting these great possibilities, we arrived at the idea of a theatre of the visual image, in which a person can express himself or herself with the utmost freedom and emotion. Our actors do not need the language of words, not because they speak in the special plastic language of mime, but because they express themselves so clearly and honestly that there is no need for words. Their acting rests on strong, direct, powerful emotions."

"But surely this is very close to clownery?"

"That's why the name of our theatre now contains these two words "clown-mime.""

"And how do you think your theatre will develop in the future?"

"Firstly, we do not propose to select any particular form as a standard for our theatre. Our motto is "Only forwards!" This interest in clownery and eccentricity has brought us success, but in fact it is not the only direction in our work. We have many productions in different genres: *Mimprovizy*, *Small Olympiada* and *Pictures from an Exhibition* based on Mussorgsky's music, *Little Boy Kibalchish*, *Petrushka* and others. As soon as we feel that our flexible forms are beginning to grow rigid, and our devices and means of expression are getting repetitive (i.e., that our main principle of "everything for love" is being violated), we immediately abandon the gate we have opened and start jumping over the fence again in search of new forms and new content.

But our greatest endurance test will come this spring. As soon as the weather gets warmer, we shall set off round the villages and towns of the Baltic with our tent. It's not the town dweller's nostalgia for the countryside, although I myself was born in the country and love it. We want to have a go at "street theatre", where everything depends on goodwill, on love, and the spectator watches the performer as long as he finds him or her interesting...

* * *

That was seven years ago.

And how everything has changed since then. Reading this interview today, you can't help wondering where it has all gone. How could it happen that the Play-Makers clown-mime theatre no longer exists? Surely they did not lose their "joyful heart"? It was all going so well...

Of the theatre studios that grew up in the eighties the Play-Makers were perhaps the only ones who managed to win not only public recognition, but almost universal affection. Adults were always imitating Lyonya Leikin's special way of saying "Stop that!", while kids at kindergarten played at being Asisyaichik's clown, and teenagers sang "Blue canaries", the song in the sketch that made Valera Keft famous (the audience even knew that his nickname was "Dandelion"). In general, the Play-Makers repertoire at that time was a household word with the members of their adoring audiences.

Unlike most theatre studios the Play-Makers never experienced financial difficulties. They began to tour abroad before the others and more frequently, thus ensuring a healthy budget. The usual language barrier did not exist for them—they did without words on the stage.

Success accompanied them abroad as well, as can be seen not only from the reviews, but also from the countless contacts which they made, personal as well as professional. With the help of their numerous new friends, the Play-Makers were able to organise in 1989 what was an unprecedented enterprise for those days, a Caravan of Peace, with street theatres from all over the world taking part. After a presentation in Moscow, the Caravan travelled round several towns in the Soviet Union and then nearly all the countries of Central Europe. Its composition changed from time to time (depending on the concrete plans of the different theatres), but the Play-Makers stayed with it from beginning to end. Their theatrical journey round the world lasted about two years, because they kept making more and more new contacts "on the way".

The price they had to pay for this apparently unconditional success was too high. The theatre broke up.

It broke up into a small group that continued to support Polunin and those who now call themselves Play-Makers minus 4.

When asked why this happened the Play-Makers' former artistic director prefers to keep silent. The team who left him offers an answer which one finds it hard to believe, however. "Slava decided to make money by organising all sorts of international festivals. But we got tired of running round the ministeries to get papers signed and pleading with people to give permission. We're actors and we want to act, to go out on the stage and talk to the audience. *Asisyai Revue* is an old programme, but we went on churning it out, travelling from one country to the next. You can make a living like that, of course, but why bother? It's so boring!"

No matter how earnestly the Play-Makers minus 4 faction explained their version to me, I couldn't help thinking that there was a different reason. Neither of the parties was to blame for their "divorce": not the petitioner nor the defendant. If anyone is to blame it is all of us, that is to say, what has been happening to us over the last few years.

The Play-Makers became successful when things were relatively stable in our country. The dubious foundations of this stability did not suit a lot of people, the Play-Makers included, but the clown masks which appeared in their theatre reflected this "stability". During the Play-Makers's absence, i.e., their two years of travelling round Europe, the life of their fellow-countrymen changed to such an extent that their old masks are now out of date. They no longer produce a response from the audience. Quite different tactics are needed now.

Perhaps it was because he understood this that the Play-Makers' former director, Polunin, decided to change his profession from actor to impresario, so as to sit out the carve-up, gain time and get used to the new situation. On his return to St Petersburg he proceeded with enviable energy to set up the Academy of Fools, which was opened in the autumn

Anvar Libabov, Valery Keft and Lyonya Leikin in *Bezsolnitsa*. Photo: P. Lebedev.

of 1992. But this is all words. As for deeds... There was the pre-Christmas carnival (December 1992), and the Silly Woman Festival (March 1993) which took place under the aegis of the Academy and were a complete flop, in spite of the fact that they were advertised all over the mass media. Polunin's two solemnly declaimed appeals for everyone to relax and enjoy themselves were not well received by the audience, which had long since lost the capacity to be light-hearted.

Play-Makers minus 4 seem to have chosen a different path. For the presentation of their "new" theatre, which took place on the stage of the House of Actors on 6 May, 1993, they prepared a new production, as is the custom. It was called *Bezsolnitsa*. In this somewhat clumsy word one can easily detect the intention to link two things: the state of a person on whom the sun is not shining ("bez solntsa") and who has insomnia ("bessonnitsa"). Not the most pleasant of conditions, to be sure!

Valerry Keft and Lyonya Leikin in *Bezsolnitsa*. Photo: P. Lebedev.

Valery Keft and Viktor Solovyov in *Bezsolnitsa*. Photo: P. Lebedev.

Each of the clown interludes which made up the Play-Makers minus 4's first production was full of black humour, which incidentally had a rather strange quality: it was as flat as tasteless distilled water which can never quench your thirst... The atmosphere produced by their acting was very different from that which each member of the audience experienced in his or her everyday life. A communing of spirits did not take place.

Nor did it take place in the film *Iron Women*, the aim of which, as the Play-Makers minus 4 themselves said, was to talk about elderly Russian women who had lived through many political regimes and were now struggling through the present one.

The appearance of this film caused some surprise, to put it mildly. The Play-Makers' old women bore a strange resemblance to Tom and Jerry in Walt Disney's famous cartoon series, a kind of horror film in which one of them, for example, starts to plaster the other on the wall, then they both get up and start chasing each other as if nothing had happened. And it's very funny!

The old women who appear in the Play-Makers' film *Iron Women* also look funny when they run, but why they are running and what all this has to do with the poor old women who can barely survive today is almost impossible to understand however hard you try.

Lyonya Leikin in *Bezsolnitsa*. Photo: P. Lebedev.

There was some restrained applause after the first showing of *Iron Women* in the St Petersburg House of Actors and a barely concealed feeling of disappointment in the audience, when suddenly onto the stage came Lyonya Leikin and proceeded to show his latest "Nasties" sketch.

He came on, sat down on a chair, pulled up his legs and put his clenched fists on his knees. And just sat there, keeping himself to himself. Just went on sitting.

Suddenly a command rang out which made not only Lyonya but the whole audience shudder. A harsh voice over the loudspeaker barked in a tone which allowed no argument: "Work!"

Lyonya jumped up and began to dig like fury. When there were no more shouts, he sat down on the chair again.

Then another command rang out:

"Rest!"

He froze to the chair, as if he was resting.

"Stand up!"
"Sit down!"
"Work!"
"Sleep!"
"Walk!"

The commands came faster and faster, more and more senseless.

And before our eyes Lyonya turned into a non-person and the audience recognised themselves in his character, worn out by the endless and meaningless changes of commands which have been barked at all of us for so many years now, like the "voice" from the loudspeaker.

And you couldn't help thinking that everything must be all right. That our Play-Makers are still alive, even though they are minus four.

True, a few weeks later their small team, which now consists of only five (Lyonya Leikin, Valery Keft, Viktor Solovyov, Anvar Libabov and Anna Orlova) went touring abroad again to carry out previously concluded contracts and sign new ones.

Their earnings are nice and healthy now, but don't get too envious of them. The actors of the Play-Makers minus 4 theatre, like most theatre studios, do not always get their pay and when they do it's not very much, because the team have decided jointly to put the lion's share of their huge earnings into building a Theatre Centre, which is scheduled to go up shortly not far from Chernyshevsky Metro Station. They are not alone in this endeavour. The Tree actors are also taking part in this project together with the Play-Makers.

Both teams have embarked on this venture in the hope of acquiring a roof over their heads in their native land.

Derevo: the Tree and its roots

The Tree (in Russian, *Derevo*) is the idol of the young.

Each of its countless admirers would give anything to be like Anton Adasinsky, the leader of this theatre group.

But the Tree is inimitable. Attempts to copy it always end in a fiasco, yet the Tree itself goes on flourishing.

The Tree is extremely popular, although ever since 1989 the theatre has spent most of its time touring abroad, with only a few rare performances in St Petersburg during brief homecomings.

The Tree is a theatre which has never put on a single play in the whole five years of its existence. They do not put on plays as a matter of principle. The dramatic fabric of their productions rests more on the non-verbal level of communication than the verbal, and they always invent it themselves.

They have two favourite forms (I am not sure they can be called genres): (1) the deep immersion in oneself which is probably found only in a state of meditation; and (2) something which is called "krutoye stebalovo" in Russian, "krutoy" being teenage slang for the superlative degree of comparison of two adjectives, namely, the best and most effective, and "stebalovo" the noun from the verb "stebat'sya", which means to laugh thinly, be ironical, or play the fool, in other words "a big laugh".

These two forms first appeared when Anton was working with the Play-Makers, and this is how it happened:

The stage is in total darkness except for the single line of pale blue rays shining from above. On the edges of this lighted strip two figures are kneeling. They have an austere, serene, almost ascetic look, their outlines blurred in the faint light. Between the two of them, hanging on a long thread is a metal ball which fits easily into their hands. The figures send the ball backwards and forwards to each other. Only the sending (or receiving) hand plays an active part. This duet lasts for a long time. The play of the hands is remarkably rich in nuances. The audience reads them like a story, no less rich and sad than Shakespeare's *Romeo and Juliet*.

The first opus in the "big laugh" series also appeared during the studio period. It is the "Taxi" sketch. It is played by two actors. One has a red carrot nose and shaved head and is dressed in a long striped bathing costume like the ones men wore at the beginning of the century. He walks round and round in a circle "all the way". His aim in life is to jog round in a circle without stopping. He is no longer a human being, but a kind of walking function. A clockwork man, in fact. He is the taxi and his hands, like tongues of flame coming out of the engine, jerk up and down

Yelena Yarovaya in the play *Search for the Female Line* at the Tree Theatre. Photo: V. Konrad.

in front of his "ugly mug": also without stopping. He was played by Anton.

The second man is carrying a case. He is dressed any old how, has one solitary tooth in his mouth, and his hair is sticking up all over the place. He is just as busy as the first man, only his job is different, namely, to stop the taxi. And he was played by Lyonya Leikin.

To the great delight of the audience this pair of idiots spends about ten minutes each trying to do what he wants: one keeps getting in front of the other only to be pushed out of the way, with a bit more force each time.

In the end they are half-dead with exhaustion, but nevertheless continue to pursue their conflicting aims. Darkness envelopes the scene of this "ideological struggle", just as the waves would have washed it away, if it were drawn in the sand. The men disappear, although they have not given up (preferring death to surrender), so the audience can easily imagine their eternal conflict continuing in the next world as well.

In the Play-Makers clown-mime studio, where Adasinsky began, they often had evenings just for "themselves" when anyone could perform anything that came into his head. They were called "Nasty-basties".

The "Taxi" sketch is from this series. But the more "Nasties" Anton produced like this, the more striking they were, and the more envious the Play-Makers' director, V. Polunin, became of him.

Anton left in the end and set up his own troupe "The Tree" a couple of years later. It consists of four people only, Tanya Khabarova, Lyonya Yarovaya, Alexei Merkulov and Anton himself, whom it was a great pleasure to interview.

"Tell us a bit about yourself, Anton."

"What shall I tell you?"

"Oh, how you got involved in the theatre, for example. It didn't happen straightaway, did it? You're thirty-three now, and the Tree is only five."

"After school I decided for fun (for a bet, actually) to go to the Constructional Engineering Institute. Everyone said it was impossible to get into an institute, but I managed it, although I left again straightaway."

"On the second of September?"

"No, I stuck it out for three months, and in the fourth I failed descriptive geometry and ran away. Ran away literally, to Asia, and began travelling around there. I went all over the place with a friend and it was very interesting. Then I came back and studied photography at the Institute of Culture. I had been really keen on photography as a kid. In 1982 it was this interest in photography that took me to the Mime Parade, where I met Slava Polunin and the other Play-Makers. I gave up the institute straightaway, of course, and a year later photography as well, because by then I had started to act. Apart from that I also learned to play the guitar when I was still at school.

At the Play-Makers for some mysterious reason Valera Keft and I became good friends straightaway. We have been inseparable ever since, although we are now working in different teams, but that doesn't matter at all. He and I thought up hundreds of sketches together! We believed in everything we did. And there was always such a fantastic degree of honesty. Our debut was in the Strange Games group. That was back in '84."

"Wait a minute. The Play-Makers clown-mime theatre had a studio. You studied theatre there, didn't you?"

"Yes, I studied there under Kirill Nikolayevich Chernozyomov. He was a great guy, of course. And he certainly revised our system of values for us!"

"Like how?"

"Well, just take the way he behaves for a start. He comes to lessons in a coat he has been wearing for so long that it's almost the same shape as he is, sits down and takes some Validol heart tablets out of his pocket, then a chess set out of a bag, and all the time he's shouting: "It's a blood-thirsty business, lads! Holding a sword in your hand is a blood-thirsty business!"

Or "You mustn't be a teddy-bear in your mother's hands!" and so on. Practically everything he says deserves to be written down.

But that's not the main thing, of course. He's a real romantic who has a special way of making contact with people. He just sits there, muttering away about something, but you understand him perfectly and a deep, special sense of communion arises. And he teaches you some important things. He shows you how essential it is to use your imagination! Say you're doing some corny study about a self-service canteen, for example. Kirill whispers to you in his famous booming voice: "Yes! Yes! So you're carrying this tray and it suddenly starts to wobble and… down it flies with your set lunch for 1 rouble 20 copecks!"

That's the sort of person Kirill Nikolayevich is. He told us that trays in Soviet canteens can fly!

Keft, Leikin and I dreamed up a mass of sketches like this, as a result of which the production "Dreams" was born."

"That was the beginning of the split in the Play-Makers, wasn't it?"

Yes, practically. Some of the kids were dying to get going, while others lazed around having a smoke. Polunin organised a debate and said we should either all join in the work or at least not form an opposition. I was still full of uncompromising ideas acquired during my youthful journeys around the country. So in reply to all of this I said "Go and get…" and simply walked out. I was really het up, of course.

Later it turned out (this is what I was told at least) that if I hadn't left so abruptly Slava would have had to go himself, and we would have stayed. A few years later some of the others did the same as me. And now they are the Play-Makers minus 4. Polunin is among the minuses.

"How did you land up in the Avia rock group?"

"I was working in films at the time. The boys from Avia came up and asked me to do a clip. So we made a very funny clip, and a show came out of it too. I knew it would be a one-off thing. They got some girls from a technical college, who had nothing but their vital statistics and were as thick as posts!"

"You took them just for their looks, did you, like they do in the cinema?"

"Yes, on the whole. This primitive material just needed to be worked on a bit to create the proper atmosphere. They were fine, those girls. In the end something strange appeared in them: shining, empty eyes with inspired primitive movements! But it was obvious they would only be good for one rock show. And our venture got out of date very quickly. Everything was changing so rapidly then. Newspaper texts were much tougher than the ones we spoke on the stage. And each day people learnt things about life (from life itself) that made the revelations of rock musicians pale by comparison.

To cut it short, the Tree was born on 15 April, 1988. Our first production was called *The region of the colour red*."

"And ever since then as soon as your name is mentioned everyone feels bound to talk about *buto*."

"You've said it! There's a great deal of discussion about *buto*, not only here but all over the world. Whereas in fact neither we nor you, nor anyone has the right to talk about *buto*, except for the two people who created it.

Buto was created by Katsu Ono and Tatsumi Michikato. It was largely connected with the history of Japan and the appearance of theatres of the atomic bomb. On the one hand, all that is not new, and on the other, it's a long story. By the end of the fifties, thanks to its two creators, *buto* became popular and began to attract attention, etc.

Tatsumi died last year of cyrrhosis of the liver, but Katsu Ono is still alive. He is eighty-six, but he still gives performances like before."

"On his own?"

"Sometimes on his own and sometimes with his son. His son is fifty-two. They can say what buto is and they do, but not in the way we are used to..."

If Katsu Ono is in the mood he talks about *buto* for a long time, emotionally, poetically and very beautifully, but always going parallel to the question. This simply means that *buto* cannot be put into words. It is a kind of island which cannot be strictly defined. Everything around us can be formulated, but the centre cannot be put into words. Everyone is familiar with *buto*. We have all experienced the silence that suddenly descends on a noisy company seated round a table, and things like that."

"So you think *buto* is not an artistic trend, but a kind of channel to reveal the depths of the soul, do you?"

"You could put it like that, but I prefer the way Katsu Ono himself defined it, or rather, how he joked his way out of it. When people go on at him to explain what *buto* is all about, he says something like this:

'One evening my friend Tatsumi Michikato came to see me with a bottle of sake. We sat for a long time, drinking the sake, looking out of the window and talking about the moon, women and horses.'

At this point he gets absorbed by this "picture" and forgets all about the person who has asked him the question.

Then there is usually a long pause and the question is repeated: 'But how did *buto* appear, maestro?'

'I've just told you!' Katsu Ono exclaims.

These days you can hear conversations about third-generation *buto*, but Katsu Ono thinks that what arose with him will disappear with him too. Everyone creates their own *buto*. Most of the so-called *buto* groups simply repeat the external form: they shave their heads, paint their bodies white and lie in a foetal pose. But this is not *buto*!"

"But you shaved your head too, didn't you?"

"Yes, I did!"

"And painted your body white and lay in a foetal pose?"

"Yes! We had to master the fundamentals. If Katsu Ono had seen us then, he would probably have said this was just pretty pictures. Yet when the maestro saw our "Horseman", where there are hardly any naked bodies, but a lot of mime, clowning and even puppets, he was very approving. And he even said it was *buto*!"

"But how did you first get to know about the stylistics of classical *buto*, if we can coin a phrase. Did you go to Japan or see it on a video?"

"No. We didn't go to Japan then, and I still don't have a video, although we watch quite a lot.

In my case it all began with some photographs that made a great impression on me. I remember there was a book with photographs of the mentally ill. Their faces were full of naked, powerful emotions! The second book was about *buto*, a tiny album with big photographs by Jacques Gailloucou. And the people on them were not prettified with any of the inventions of modern civilisation. Then we simply started to use our imagination in the same strain. And this was a great shock to the public."

"Do you believe that theatregoers should be given a shock? Can't they be treated in some other way?"

"We didn't set out specially to shock the audience. We simply did what we wanted to do, but this upset a lot of people. Incidentally the newspapers made much more of this shock that it was in fact. Then under the pretext of discussing *buto* there was endless talk about us. This primitive habit of calling anything that gives you a shock *buto* had already developed in Europe by then and got as far as us. Ten naked women carrying a log round the stage is *buto*; some people hanging upside down from a skyscraper (one of whom falls to his death) is *buto*; photographs of naked bodies and people with shaved heads in a primitive pop album is *buto*; somebody performing a macabre dance is also *buto*. We don't like that sort of *buto*.

I think the best way to end a conversation on this subject is to say that *buto* doesn't exist."

"But it does, doesn't it?"

"Yes, it does. It is inside everyone, if they do not kill their very self and if they live each moment of their lives as only they can. Whether a person is good or bad is not so important. The important thing is that

The Horseman at the Tree Theatre. Photo: V. Konrad.

he or she is what he or she is. This kind of *"buto*-person" does not betray himself or herself, but finds himself or herself ... always and everywhere.

Yet this is rare today and very hard to achieve. Most of the time our theatres simply concentrate on form, external attributes."

The Horseman at the Tree Theatre. Photo: V. Konrad.

"Are you perhaps referring to "DO-TEATR"?"

"Yes, I am. I thought very highly of them when they were beginning, but then they went off somewhere…"

"Why did you go off to Czechoslovakia?"

"Why do you think?"

"I think it was because our theatres were having a hard time."

"Everyone seems to think that, but we never had any particular difficulties. Our productions went on every day and played to full houses. We toured abroad and earned enough money to pay for renting the Leningrad Youth Palace. It's just that we got the travel bug or, as we also say, the touring syndrome."

"What did you actually do in Czechoslovakia?"

"Looked after our things. We didn't just sit around there. We were travelling all the time. In Prague we were based at the Theatre on Zabralli, which was directed by Turba after Fialka died. We rehearsed there for about three months. Just when we felt ready to leave, a two-year contract arrived. Everything worked out beautifully. None of the team had any doubts about whether to go or not. We left almost straightaway. It was an interesting moment, although in Prague we had perfect hothouse conditions for cultivating roses…"

"Then why do you bother to leave those hothouse conditions from time to time and return to our "neglected garden"? For private reasons or are you just homesick?"

"We don't divide our life into private and public. For us the theatre is our main private motif. When we went away from here two-and-a-half years ago, I left my mother, my sister and my nephew. That's not a problem. It's either one thing or the other. Either you decide to sit by a child's bedside or you go out and do something."

"That's a rather harsh way of putting it! But, tell me, have you come home for good now, or is this just a visit?"

"We are at home everywhere and we're visitors everywhere too!"

"You'll soon be telling me that we are all visitors on this Earth of ours. I didn't ask you about that."

"We will always go touring. For the time being mostly "over there", because we need to earn money, a lot of money. Together with the Play-Makers minus 4 we want to get on with setting up a Theatre Centre and building it by Metro Chernyshevskaya. The project has already swallowed up several million. How much more will be required, we don't yet know, but we want to get our own home!

So we've come back and been here for quite a long time, but as for our performances, you know what that's been like, two or three times here and there without any publicity. No real creativity and no real money. The reason is very simple: it's bad management. We have no guarantee that if we announce performances each day (of the "Horseman", for example), we shall get a full house. We would be only too happy to revive "The region of red", and do a new production, and act some street plays, and work flat out!

Look at Theatre Bouffe, which is a load of rubbish, in my opinion. They play to full houses every day, simply because they have their own stage and good publicity. We still haven't managed to solve this problem. Each time we sally out into the town ourselves to put up a few posters, people say: "Ugh! That's the Tree again with its antediluvian methods." I keep thinking that if we put on a completely new production and want to perform it often, we must make sure that the whole town knows about it. It's no fun acting a first night to a half-empty auditorium."

"Assuming that this organisational question will be solved, do you have the strength, energy and desire to perform each day?"

"No, we don't. Very few theatres use up as much energy as the Tree in each performance. What is more, we don't have (and never will have) understudies, so no replacements are possible. Our regime is like the ballet, where no one dances each day. The best possible regime for us is three days working and two days off. Or else to put on a production that doesn't require so much energy and alternate it with the others.

If we get a hall at the Chernyshevskaya, we'll start working with the regime of a repertoire theatre."

"Will all the Tree's future production be made according to the "patchwork quilt" principle?"

"In what sense?"

"In the sense that your productions not only do not rest on any literary foundation, but always consist of individual "pieces" which remind one sometimes of a novella or sketch and sometimes of a kind of blitz. You seem to steer clear of full-length forms.

How do your productions arise?"

"The moment comes when everyone, without consulting one another, feels that it is time for a new work."

"And then what?"

"Everyone starts doing something on their own, preparing some kind of 'etude'. And the production grows out of them."

"That's precisely what I mean, that your productions have the structure of a collage. However hard you try it's impossible to detect any kind of single dramatic action which develops from the beginning to the end in them."

"We're not striving for that. Firstly, because life today is itself highly eclectic. Surely you wouldn't find it interesting to talk about the same thing for two hours in a row?"

"It depends on what. For example, I watched a film of Peter Brook's "Mahabharata" which lasted for three-and-a-half hours (they say the play goes on for nine hours) and it was very interesting!"

"Oh, well, Peter Brook! There are very few examples like that today. They are the exception rather than the rule. And that film was made some time ago. Today people respond to something different, I think."

"What is that?"

"Today we all exist in a very concentrated way. Our time is condensed to the extreme. This, I believe, explains why the form of the clip appeared. The clip is not just for making an advertisement. Remember Parker's film *The Wall*? That's a clip that goes on for an hour-and-a-half. And our life today is a clip. Look how we communicate, how we talk to one another. Ten to fifteen words in a sentence, no compound or complex sentences, and we keep jumping from one subject to another.

See?"

"Yes, I see."

"That's it then."

* * *

The Tree is the idol of the young.

You hardly ever see adults at a Tree production…

Diklon flickers on

The Diklon theatre studio first appeared in 1989. The word "Diklon" does not actually mean anything in any language. According to Yuri Kretov, the theatre studio's director, they chose it because it sounded nice. And its repertoire opened with a production called *Flickering*.

You could also use the word "flickering" to describe the studio's subsequent way of life: putting on a performance at some state establishment then disappearing out of sight for a long time.

They tried a couple of times to organise regular performance on hired stages, of which there are more than enough in St Petersburg, but it just didn't work. The atmosphere in these places is "not right", and the conditions of the boxlike stage are not suitable for putting Diklon's creative ideas into practice.

Flickering needs the tension and magic of a circle, which is made up of members of the audience and encloses the "action" taking place in the performing area. In other words, it requires an unusual organisation of space, because here the very device of the actor's existence is based on interaction with space. Peter Brook's words "A person moves around in space, somebody watches him, and that is already enough to produce theatrical action" apply to *Flickering* perfectly.

In this programme production of Diklon's several people move around in space, sometimes on their own, sometimes in twos or threes, or all together.

The actors do not act any concrete social or everyday subjects in front of us. They are simple men and women dressed in long black robes. The rich folds of the material drape each of the figures in a special manner, but in spite of this one has a sense of inner unity, because both the colour and the principle of treating the costumes are identical. They are a kind of "uniform", which is what makes the audience regard the people "moving in space" in an abstract way.

Yet this is certainly not an expressionist version of "man per se" generalised almost to the point of allegory. What we see before us (and we, the audience, very quickly enter into the fantasy offered by the theatre) are not material beings at all. They are human souls, so to say, although this is certainly not meant to be the realm of the dead. They are the souls of living people who are wandering around the space of life.

It is the way in which these most unusual stage characters move that enables and even compels us to assume this. At this point a short "technical" description might be useful.

The actors have been trained in such a way that their hands are capable of existing separately from the rest of their body, as it were. At

The Diklon Theatre's *Flickering*.

first it is their groping hands that inscribe all sorts of geometrical figures in space, creating a kind of sketch which contains a trajectory of that particular person's forthcoming movements in his life space. The movements of the hands are what is "desired". After what is "desired" has taken possession of a person, it tries to realise itself in what is "real", but in the ensuing clash with unforeseen obstacles, the "desired" is transformed into formless "chaos" and exists up to the point when a new desire appears in the person's soul. This is the general scheme for everyone on the stage, but the rhythm and tempo are different in each case.

Developing gradually in space and time a picture is formed on the stage which records the lines of people "supra-social" relations. Relations exclusively on the level of emotional and spiritual communication. This picture enchants one by its originality and depth. Without high-flown speeches, offensive abuse, or the slightest attempt at realistic description, we understand how this duet arose and that triangle fell apart, why that particular soul is wandering alone, while others long for solitude, remaining estranged... The content of this production grows directly out of its form: archetypal models of inter-personal relations replace one another, finding short-lived embodiment in the ephemeral material of movement, only to be destroyed by movement too.

It must be added that the audience responds not only to the unusual problems of the conversation offered by Diklon and not only to the unique system of movement invented inside this theatre, but also to the production's rhythmical base.

Flickering is acted in complete silence, occasionally broken by the sound of a voice singing somewhere off-stage, a real voice, of course, not a recording. The main rhythm-forming element is the sound of footsteps which comes from the constant moving around of bare-footed people on the stage. The sound of their footsteps is intensified by the ringing of the little bells tied round their ankles.

I hope all this will make it clear that in its productions Diklon strives for communication with the audience on a level which is pre-verbal and extra-verbal, clearly acting in the spirit of the ideas of Antonin Artaud, one of the precursors of the twentieth-century theatre, who believed that the theatre had a language of its own. This "specific language of the stage" cannot be reduced to the dialogue form of expounding this or that content. On the contrary, it is capable of attaining the heights of poetry and making use of the active impact of such means of expression as plasticity, pantomime, mime, gesture, music, dance, sound, intonation, architecture and lighting, in short, everything that is capable of enlivening and filling the "empty space" of the stage.

The actors at the Diklon theatre studio are searching for the "specific language of the stage". The public at large knows practically nothing of their activity. It is not even aware of their existence. But professionals, who adopt a somewhat cautious but "must see it" approach to the "laboratory experiments" by Yuri Kretov (a graduate from the direction faculty of the Krupskaya Institute) come to all its performances and then discuss what they have seen animatedly for a long time...

Eduard Bersudsky's kinemats at the Sharmanka Theatre.

What we have we don't treasure, when we lose it, we cry[1]

The Sharmanka ("Barrel Organ") theatre is different. The actors here are large wooden mechanical toys or kinemats, as they are called.

The first audience reaction to Sharmanka's appearance in the city was a fairly stereotyped one: "Mechanical toys!" It sent parents hurrying off to the theatre with their children, particularly as the theatre presentation was shown on Petersburg television on New Year's Eve 1990, when the school holidays had just begun.

The children liked the idea of going to see toys at the theatre, but did not take to the kinemats, because they seemed too full of adult worries, not happy enough.

When the hullabaloo about the opening of a new "children's" theatre had died down, Sharmanka was flooded by Intourist groups. The foreign visitors were ecstatic. They had never seen anything like it, even at the famous Georges Pompidou centre!

The visitors' book acquired a vast number of exotic entries in foreign languages: "There's nothing like your theatre anywhere else in the world", "Marvellous!", "Fantastic!" and so on and so forth.

But soon the enthusiastic stream of foreign tourists began to dry up (not in relation to Sharmanka, but in general). The growing instability in our country made foreigners less keen to visit it.

While Sharmanka was experiencing the ups-and-downs of fortune, Petersburg theatre critics were at a loss, preferring to keep silent about it. For two years there was not a single sensible article about it in the city periodicals. Only information as to what, where and when.

None of the Sharmankars (and there are only two at the helm) were in the slightest put out by all this. By then both Eduard Bersudsky and Tatiana Zhakovskaya were used to doing everything themselves. They even wrote about themselves (Tatiana Zhakovskaya didn't graduate from the theatre criticism faculty of the Theatre Institute for nothing!). In fact they wrote and printed the most interesting of all the booklets that came out about the numerous theatre studios which sprang up in St Petersburg in the late eighties and early nineties. Here is the text:

WHO NEEDS THIS THEATRE?

A few years ago the idea of opening a new theatre, particularly one that was different, was quite unthinkable.

---

[1]a Russian folk saying.

Today, in the age of intellectual ferment and universal bedlam known in the West by the name of "perestroika", you can open anything you like. Surviving is highly problematic, however.

But kindly tell me who needs the theatre nowadays, when our whole life, from dawn to dusk, is one long play with an infinite number of people taking part and such a crazy mixture of events from different genres that you can't help suspecting the director of lacking any sense of taste. The finale of this production which is playing everywhere at the same time, is so unpredictable that the most people ever dream of is having an interval in the form of a good sleep without any dreams.

And the fact that Eduard Bersudsky's kinemats, after moving on the eve of 1990 from a cramped room to the respectable premises of a former kindergarten, are still turning their wheels and even multiplying is a miracle that has taken place thanks to a lot of people:

– who give up their modest offerings to Sharmanka;
– who bring us the wire, wheels, motors, funny scraps of iron and bits of old furniture from which the kinemats are made;
– the theatregoers from Germany who printed our posters;
– everyone who works in our theatre, permanently or periodically, for nothing or for a purely symbolic wage;
– the executive committee of Moscow district council and its chairman Valery Ivanovich Malyshev, thanks to whom we have a roof over our heads and even the money for our first tour;
– Professor Jerry Janiček from the University of Kentucky, who was our very first sponsor;
– the actors and musicians from the Four Windows amateur theatre with whom I managed to survive the years of stagnation fairly well. While the Master was making kinemats in his "ecological niche", we were acting Shakespeare, Williams, Beckett, Schwartz, Volodin and Zlotnikov in ours. We talked about what we liked and read what we found interesting. Perestroika and glasnost' did not come as a shock for them. They did not learn very much that was new. Meetings and demonstrations bored them, so they rolled up their sleeves and founded Sharmanka;
– the Leningrad (now Petersburg) journalists who managed to attract the attention of the old, totally undemocratic and unprogressive city bosses to the fate of the Master and his work;
– the street theatres Dog Troupe from Holland, Nucleo from Italy and Footsborne from Great Britain who, in the summer of 1980 at the Caravan for Peace festival confirmed what we had always thought: that today, like centuries ago, the theatre can be not so much a profession as a way of life;

– that fine man, mathematician and poet Vitya Shvartz, who first took me to the Master's den. He was our friend and we all agreed that one day we would go for a walk along the Champs Elysee together. But fate willed otherwise. A year ago Vitya sang his last songs in our theatre, and today is he walking (through the Elysian fields) in a different world, which may be better than ours.

In helping such a strange theatre in such an unsuitable age these people, or so it seems to me, are guided by an intuitive sense that the Master's works do not belong to the present day alone. But perhaps the reason is that kinemats are made from things that have been thrown on the scrap heap. And periodically people try to scrap things that will be essential for us tomorrow.

Tatiana Zhakovskaya
director and producer

(In a separate column the writer Marietta Turian gives a brief account of the Master's life):

Eduard Bersudsky, one of the most original artists of the Leningrad underground, has not had an easy life.

Bersudsky was born in Leningrad in 1939. As a young man he tried various ways of earning a living without special training. He worked in a mine in the Far North, in Vorkuta, served in the army there for three years, then returned to Leningrad where he was a driver, plumber, carpenter, sailor, skipper on a barge and stoker.

Not until the age of twenty-five did he decide to devote himself to wooden sculpture. Bersudsky rejected the opportunity to get an artistic education at an official educational establishment, the Academy of Arts, but received an excellent professional training in the workshop of Boris Vorobyov, a well-known sculptor of the older generation. At the same time he worked in the sphere of wooden park sculpture.

It was around this period that he developed his aesthetic and philosophical views, his keen artistic eye and unexpected, sometimes staggering vision of the world. The artistic means chosen by the Master to embody his ideas were equally original—sculpted wooden kinemats.

At that time, when the West was learning about Russian life from the political or poetic sarcasms of Alexander Solzhenitsyn and Josef Brodsky, Bersudsky was creating his artistic and philosophical version of the Soviet absurd in the limited space of his small Leningrad flat. The world which he created over several decades is a Theatre of Life, in which eternal and topical themes, scathing, bitter irony, fearlessness and wisdom are closely intertwined.

The age of so-called perestroika has changed little in the Master's outlook. In reflecting on his country he remains true to the ideas of historical scepticism.

* * *

Bersudsky makes his kinemats from bits and pieces that have been thrown on the scrap heap! That is to say, from the remains of our everyday culture! And this is perhaps what creates the secret contained within them, their powerful magnetic field.

By finding refuge in the Master's kinemats, these familiar objects acquire a meaning similar to Hoffmann's phantasmogoria. Take a look at this fragment of one of them, for example. Some worn boots are standing by a rickety chair painted white. On the chair is an accordion and next to it a pood weight hanging on a thick chain. When the kinemat begins to work, the weight starts going up and down, up and down noisily, the accordion emits some naive musical sounds, and the boots tap recklessly in time with it.

There is something about this "scene" that is painfully familiar to each of us. It is not so long since we were all bellowing "With songs we struggle and we win…", whereas in fact we were practically destitute.

Each fragment like this has its own mini-programme which in turn is part of the general programme for the whole kinemat. The actions of all the kinemats working in the production are logically coordinated. All the productions at the Sharmanka theatre are organised on this principle.

The kinemat with the boots, chair, accordion and weight (and plenty more besides) takes part, inter alia, in the production *Proletarian Greetings to Jean Tengel from the master E. Bersudsky in the Cradle of Three Revolutions*. It is about concrete events in our country's history.

The Sharmanka theatre's first production was *The Wheel* which interpreted life as such on a philosophical level. The kinemats here look quite different. They are wooden sculptures of impressive dimensions (two-and-a-half metres high) or wooden structures decorated with sculpture. One of them, for example, is inset with small figures revolving in a circle. Each of them represents a stage in life (from the infant in its mother's arms to the Reaper with the scythe). It is actually called "Life".

The Master, solitary, no longer in his prime, childless and having just buried his mother, works on his kinemats from dawn to dusk. He has now made about two hundred of them. They are as greedy and capricious as children: first they want screws, then they need to be painted or oiled, or they have a screw missing and where will you find one now? Only at a second-hand market and only for an astronomical amount of money. The most expensive item is electricity, of course, which they just eat up.

Neither their "father", the master Bersudsky, nor their "god-mother", Tatiana Zhakovskaya, has any capital or any hope of inheriting some. So they have gone on a long foreign tour with their Sharmanka, from festival to festival.

And they're not likely to return, because there is nowhere to come back to. What is more, Tatiana Zhakovskaya's children and grand-children (real ones, not wooden ones) have been waiting for her for a whole year in Israel where they have gone to live permanently.

So Petersburg used to have its Sharmanka, but not any more. Only the legend remains and the song that rings in our ears "Oh, parting, parting, to a far-off land…"

Postscript

As a result of an opinion poll conducted among the inhabitants of Moscow and St Petersburg by the sociological service of the Russian Statistical Board the following information was obtained. During the period from 1992 to 1993 less than 1% of the population paid even one visit to the theatre.

This figure seems so incredible that at first you can hardly believe it. Particularly since you see a somewhat different picture if you are a frequent theatregoer.

There can be no doubt that there has been a significant drop in visiting the theatre. At ordinary performances the halls are often only half full at the very best.

The reasons for this are so obvious that they are announced over the mass media every day, like the weather forecast, in the following brief formulae: 1) the unprecedented impoverishment of the vast majority of the population, and 2) a deterioration in the criminogenic situation.

Both statements could be painted red and illustrated with masses of striking examples. But it should suffice to picture the "ordinary Russian" who is by no means certain that he or she will manage to get home safely after the play and even less certain of what the future holds in store, in order to understand why he or she has stopped going to the theatre where the price of tickets (like everything else) has risen so dramatically.

The average St Petersburgian goes to the theatre very rarely these days. He or she has too many other things on his or her mind.

Increasingly often one finds people from other towns in the audience, who are usually referred to as "guests to the city on the Neva". Visiting Russians on the whole prefer the really well-known theatres, such as the Alexandrinsky, the Bolshoi Drama Theatre and the Comedy Theatre. Tourists with more to spend go to what they regard as the more prestigious Maly Drama Theatre directed by Lev Dodin, and foreign tourists to the musical theatres (which is only natural), particularly the Marinsky.

The somewhat motley "beau monde" (ranging from "new Russians" to genuine intellectuals) is to be seen at all the first nights, of course.

But none of this concerns "ordinary St Petersburgians", of whom there are five million. So the Statistical Board's figure quoted above probably does reflect the real state of affairs.

All the more valuable then are the efforts of the new theatre studios, who are busy forming a generation of true and devoted theatre-lovers.

Index

Other titles in the Russian Theatre Archive series: